Toward a
Creative
Chaplaincy

Toward a Creative Chaplaincy

Edited by

LAWRENCE E. HOLST, S.T.M.

Director of Pastoral Care
Lutheran General Hospital
Park Ridge, Illinois

and

HAROLD P. KURTZ, M.S.

Director of Public Relations
Lutheran General Hospital
Park Ridge, Illinois

With a Foreword by

Carroll A. Wise, S.T.B., Th.D.

Professor of Pastoral Psychology and Counseling
Garret Theological Seminary
Evanston, Illinois

CHARLES C THOMAS • PUBLISHER
Springfield • Illinois • U.S.A.

Published and Distributed Throughout the World by

CHARLES C THOMAS • PUBLISHER

Bannerstone House

301-327 East Lawrence Avenue, Springfield, Illinois, U.S.A.

© *1973, by* CHARLES C THOMAS • PUBLISHER

ISBN 0-398-02673-4

Library of Congress Catalog Card Number: 72-88446

Printed in the United States of America

ROO-2

CONTRIBUTORS

Arthur O. Bickel, M.Th.: Associate Director, Department of Pastoral Care, Lutheran General Hospital

Bruce M. Hartung, Ph.D.: Associate Director, Community Counseling Center, Lutheran General Hospital.

Lawrence E. Holst, S.T.M.: Director, Department of Pastoral Care, Lutheran General Hospital

John E. Keller: Administrative Director, Rehabilitation Center, Lutheran General Hospital

Harold P. Kurtz, M.S.: Director of Public Relations, Lutheran General Hospital

Ronald R. Leslie: Associate Director, Department of Pastoral Care, Lutheran General Hospital

Harold S. Nasheim: Staff Chaplain, Department of Pastoral Care, Lutheran General Hospital Park Ridge, Illinois

Armand Nordgren: Staff Chaplain, Department of Pastoral Care, Lutheran General Hospital

Arthur J. Ree: Staff Chaplain, Department of Pastoral Care, Lutheran General Hospital

E. Alan Richardson: Consultant, Department of Pastoral Care, Lutheran General Hospital

Willard Wagner: Staff Chaplain, Department of Pastoral Care, Lutheran General Hospital

Carroll A. Wise, Th.D.: Professor of Pastoral Psychology and Counseling, Garrett Theological Seminary, Evanston, Illinois

*To the adventure of Human Ecology and those who have shared
in it, especially*
*Naurice M. Nesset and Fredric M. Norstad who envisioned it;
the Lutheran General board of trustees who nurtured it;
the late Chaplain Carl R. Nowack who lived it.*

FOREWORD

OUR task here is to put this book in something of a historical perspective in relation to the literature in the field of pastoral care.

Pastoral care of the ill and of others in various kinds of trouble and suffering has been a concern of the pastor since even before the early days of the church. The history of pastoral care is traced in considerable detail by John T. McNeil in his book *A History of the Cure of Souls.* McNeil was, in his day, a leading church historian. Two authors, one writing again from the point of view of a church historian, and the other from the point of view of modern pastoral care, have given us *Pastoral Care in a Historical Perspective.* This book is unusually good in relating insights both from history and from modern practice.

More specifically in terms of the modern hospital chaplaincy, the present volume takes its place with a rather imposing series. It should be mentioned first, however, that modern pastoral care either in hospitals or in parishes is rooted in the clinical pastoral training movement which began back in the mid 1920's. From that time on, pastoral care became a subject for critical study and not just for intuitive insights.

The first book of a group we shall mention was published in 1936. Its author was the founder of the clinical pastoral training movement, Anton Boisen. Its title was *The Exploration of the Inner World.* This book centered on the problems of mental illness and a religious understanding of the experiences of the mentally ill. It has a definite relationship to one of the chapters in the present volume.

In the same year appeared *The Art of Ministering to the Ill* by Richard Cabot and Russell Dicks. Dr. Cabot was also one of the founders of the clinical pastoral training movement. Russell Dicks was one of the early students in the movement and wrote this book when he was the chaplain of a large general hospital in Boston. A comparison of that book with the present volume will give some understanding of the distance which this movement has made in some forty years.

In 1942 there appeared a book entitled *Religion In Illness and Health* by Carroll A. Wise. Wise was Boisen's successor in Worcester State Hospital chaplaincy. In this volume, Dr. Wise attempted to relate mental illness to religion through the concepts of the organismic point of view on the one hand, and symbolic expression on the other. The chapter in the present volume on the use of religious questions has a relation to the earlier volume.

In 1960 there appeared a book entitled *Spiritual Therapy,* by Richard K. Young and Albert L. Meiburg. This book stressed the emotional and spiritual needs of various types of patients that are found in the general hospital. In 1963 Carl J. Sherzer authored *Ministering to the Physically Sick.* This book grew out of the author's hospital chaplaincy experience.

In 1961 a hospital chaplain, Granger E. Westberg, wrote *The Minister and Doctor Meet.* This was an attempt to deal with the relationships of the pastor and the physician as they met on the hospital wards. Wayne Oates has authored a number of books growing out of his experience in the clinical pastoral education movement and in the hospital chaplaincy as well as teaching in a theological school. Perhaps the one most closely related to this volume is *The Christian Pastor,* published in 1967.

There are many other authors whose works might be mentioned. Some of these deal with various aspects of the pastoral ministry while others would deal with the training of pastors, particularly clinical pastoral education. Some would have a theological stance. Space does not permit us to be exhaustive here; hence, we shall refrain.

A word about reading the present volume. It should be read as an attempt on the part of a number of pastors to interpret their work, rather than being read as a manual for pastoral care. One of the basic principles of the clinical pastoral education movement was that one learns to deal with people in trouble not just by reading or going through an intellectual process. One learns this much more profoundly through actual experience.

This experience, however, must be carefully supervised in order to bring out its values. Thus, one does not learn to be a pastor by reading a book. On the other hand, there is a value in knowing how some other pastors understand and interpret their work. Throughout this volume the personal equation far beyond the concepts or techniques will be felt by the reader. Perhaps it will stimulate the reader, be he pastor or layman, to examine his own self-understanding, including his own religious faith.

Laymen should read this book and even study it as a way of discovering the possibilities of the pastoral ministry for themselves if and when they become patients in a hospital.

The book has a deep message for pastors. Hospital administrators will discover in it a statement of the meaning of a chaplaincy program in an institution. When it comes to a modern chaplaincy program, some church-related hospitals are still back where all hospitals were before 1930. Teachers in theological schools may glean some ideas out of this volume if they are at all open-minded. Theological education again has been very slow to grasp the meaning of the approaches represented in this volume. There has been much lip service but little real integration into the seminary curriculum.

Perhaps also, some denominational officers and leaders may gain insights here which will help them to give up the antiquated idea that a man is not in the pastoral ministry unless he is the pastor of a church that is located on a corner and has a spire. There is a sense in which the opportunity for pastoral care within a modern hospital is far greater than the opportunity in a local parish, since many people will open themselves to help when they are suffering in a way in which they will not when they are not suffering. From many points of view then this volume is well worth careful reading.

CARROLL A. WISE

PREFACE

THIS book is a bit unusual. It is edited by a pastor and by a layman. But perhaps it is also symbolic of the Department of Pastoral Care at Lutheran General Hospital – a program which was developed by another pastor and by another layman.

When in the mid-1950's, the founders of Lutheran General Hospital discussed the idea of building a new hospital, the question they asked was, "Is there a place for the church-related hospital in today's society?"

The answer they found was, "No, there isn't – unless the church-related hospital can make a distinct and unique contribution." Out of this conviction Lutheran General Hospital grew, a hospital in which the chaplain has perhaps a greater degree of responsibility than he has in any other hospital.

The responsibility comes not in the running of the hospital, but in the degree of freedom with which the chaplain can function. Such an atmosphere (or ecology) exists only because clergy and laity alike recognize the value of such a program. Such a program of pastoral care does not evolve by itself. It happened only because of a variety of factors. There was, first and foremost, leadership which recognized the necessity and desirability of such a program.

There was a willingness on the part of church officials to aid in implementing a program of this nature.

There has been the continued backing and support by the hospital management, recognizing that the chaplains are performing a vital function within the hospital and that the Department of Pastoral Care is a professional department ranking with other departments of the hospital.

Because this is recognized by hospital trustees and management, acceptance comes naturally from other areas of the hospital –

nurses, physicians, therapists and the whole host of other personnel who keep the modern hospital running.

It is no accident that such a department developed at Lutheran General. There is the heritage of the Deaconesses who built the mother hospital of Lutheran General — Lutheran Deaconess Hospital. The spirit and dedication of the Deaconesses provided the foundation on which the Department of Pastoral Care was built.

Since the first clinical pastoral care education residents began their duties in 1959, more than 100 clergymen have participated in the program. Individually and collectively they have given generously of their time and talents to help make the program what it is today.

Providing the overall guidance was a visionary Board of Governors of the Lutheran Institute of Human Ecology, the parent organization of Lutheran General Hospital. Through this board, a dynamic relationship has been maintained between the church and the hospital. Working closely with the governors has been the hospital's Board of Trustees which has provided the continued support for the department.

Another source of strength to the department has been the volunteers of Lutheran General Hospital — men, women and teenagers.

But most of all, to the patients — past and present — who continue to be the best and most understanding of all teachers for the members of the Department of Pastoral Care.

This book attempts to show how the interrelated parts of a chaplaincy department can function when such a department is given the support and understanding of board, administration and professional staff members. In this book we have attempted to demonstrate the various areas in which a chaplain can function, to show how he relates to other strata of the hospital and to show how the chaplain can participate with other professionals as they work together in therapy, education and research.

It should be emphasized that chaplains do not work in a vacuum. Without the interest, support and concern of others, they would not be able to conduct any portion of their work. But through the cooperation of physicians, nurses, aides, orderlies, therapists, students, dietitians, housekeepers and the whole host of men and women who serve in the hospital, an effective ministry can be conducted.

It is in this context that this book has been written. It is our hope that through this book a more effective chaplaincy program can be nurtured in other institutions and through this hopefully will come better care for the patients. It is to this ideal that the Department of Pastoral Care is dedicated.

For one of the editors, the department has been where he has labored for the better part of his pastoral career, starting as a resident in clinical pastoral education and moving up as director of the department.

For the other editor, the pastoral care department has been an area in which most of his experience has been that of a close observer, of a friend of many of the members and as one who has appreciated the contributions made to the well-being of the hospital.

It is our feeling that this particular book could only have been written at this hospital. Both editors are appreciative for the opportunity to be able to work in such a setting. Perhaps this book can help show the appreciation we have for the people who make up Lutheran General Hospital.

HAROLD P. KURTZ
LAWRENCE E. HOLST

ACKNOWLEDGMENTS

The editors acknowledge with a deep sense of gratitude the many who have made this book possible. Our special thanks and appreciation are expressed to the following:

To the Office of the President at Lutheran General Hospital — Naurice M. Nesset, Ph.D., Alexander N. Ruggie, M.D., and Theodor L. Jacobsen, FACHA.

To R. J. Hildreth, Ph.D., chairman of the education and publication committee, for his cooperation.

To all those associated with the Department of Pastoral Care who labored long and diligently in their writing.

To Carroll A. Wise, Th.D., for his many contributions and suggestions.

To Mrs. Margaret Mendenhall and Mrs. Eve Bowman, secretaries in pastoral care, for their work.

To Mrs. Ruth Berg, secretary in public relations, for the endless typing and retyping which she has again done so well.

To Grace Kurtz, for her excellent editing, proofreading, critical reading, and constant encouragement.

To all others who aided in making this book a reality.

L.E.H.
H.P.K.

CONTENTS

Page

Foreword — *Carroll A. Wise* ix
Preface xiii
Acknowledgments xvii

Chapter

I. The Chaplain Today — *Lawrence E. Holst* 3
II. The Initial Call — *Bruce M. Hartung* 15
III. Crisis Chaplaincy — *Ronald R. Leslie* 22
IV. Ministering to the Surgical Patient — *Arthur J. Ree* 33
V. Ministering to Coronary Patients and Their Families
   — *Arthur O. Bickel* 42
VI. Pastoral Care for Patients in a Physical Medicine and
   Rehabilitation Unit — *Armand Nordgren* 55
VII. Emotions and Illness — *Harold S. Nasheim* 63
VIII. Pastoral Care of the Psychiatric Patient — *Willard Wagner* 78
IX. Chaplaincy to Alcoholics — *John E. Keller* 87
X. Ministering to Staff — *Arthur O. Bickel* and *Bruce M. Hartung* . 96
XI. The Hospital Chaplain and the Parish Pastor
   — *Lawrence E. Holst* 105
XII. A Community Pastoral Counseling Center
   — *Lawrence E. Holst* 118
XIII. The Religious Interview as a Method for Teaching
   Psychodynamics — *E. Alan Richardson* 128
XIV. The Chaplain of the Future — *Carroll A. Wise* 138
   Appendix 150
   Index 155

Toward a
Creative
Chaplaincy

"meaningful"

failitate ^ adaptation of staff, family
& patient to environment of illness.

self worth
  guilt-conscience
  anger-defense
(dependency)
  identity
  personal power
  feelings
belonging-environment

community resource person for

total health - pastoral

spiritual care

Jung

Monroe

Frankel

Rogers

Tournier

Dobhitt-religion problems
Pastors
community mental health.

I

THE CHAPLAIN TODAY

LAWRENCE E. HOLST

Because of our love for you we were ready to share with you not only
the Good News from God, but even our own lives.

I Thessalonians 2:8*

A mediator, a *mobilizer*, an *enabler* — that is the
hospital chaplain today.

As a *mediator* he is "a connecting link," an intermediary who
stands between the patient and his own feelings about his illness;
between the patient and his fellow patient; between the patient
and his family; between the patient and the world outside the
hospital; between the patient and God.

As a *mobilizer* he is one who helps to put into motion, to
summon and to activate the healing resources both within and
between persons.

As an *enabler* he facilitates, legitimizes the growth and
expression of dedication, faithfulness and concern.

The hospital chaplain today is well-trained for his task. Besides
college and seminary education, he has probably spent at least one
year in supervised clinical pastoral education, a process that
focuses on individual and professional growth. If he is a
Protestant, he is probably accredited by the American Protestant
Hospital Association's College of Chaplaincy which certifies his
professional competency.

WHAT HE IS NOT

The chaplain's role today is extremely broad and varied. It is
difficult to assign him a job description.

He is, of course, an ordained clergyman; yet he spends a small

Good News for Modern Man. The New Testament in today's English version.

percentage of his time doing what people ordinarily see pastors doing: preaching, teaching, and publicly administering the Sacraments.

He does considerable individual counseling, yet he is not a psychiatrist; he relates to families and the social mileu of the patient, yet he is not a social worker.

He prays with and conducts worship for many in the hospital, yet he is nobody's parish pastor.

Employees seek him out with their gripes and conflicts — both personal and situational — yet he is not a personnel director.

He frequently represents the hospital at community functions and in civic organizations, yet he is not a public relations director.

He may organize patients into groups, yet he is not responsible for their medical management.

He is not any of these, yet he is all of them.

The hospital chaplain is of the church, and yet he is not identified with a particular denomination. To patients and staff he represents whatever religion represents to them and to that extent he is everybody's pastor. Because his ministry ordinarily ends when hospitalization ends, many patients feel freer to express their feelings about religion to him and feel less pressure to maintain some kind of creedal conformity.

Though he is a member of the hospital staff, he is not ordinarily seen as part of the medical management and thus carries less defensiveness into situations where medical care has failed, or has been felt by the patient and/or family to have been mismanaged.

Unlike his professional colleagues, he has almost complete access to all patients, with or without their invitation. This broad accessibility exposes him to an almost endless variety of situations and an almost equally endless variety of expectations.

He is surrounded by associates whose tasks are carefully delineated and measured, while much of his work is subjective and its effects almost impossible to predict or measure. His work of quiet listening and talking seems at times out of place in an institution characterized by activity and scientific preciseness. He walks from room to room with virtually no equipment, with no intention of charting, measuring, diagnosing or prescribing anything.

WHAT HE IS

At his best, the hospital chaplain tries to help people experience God's love. He does this in ways that are as varied and manifold as God's love. At times he does it through prayer; on other occasions it might come through his reading familiar words of Scripture; for still others that love is most graphically experienced by tasting, touching, smelling, ingesting Christ's Body and Blood in the Sacrament of Communion; for many that love is experienced also when one comes into contact with quiet listening and felt human concern.

To some patients the deepest experience of God's love is to feel that he has been heard and understood and respected as a distinct, unique human being and that his suffering has at least in some small way been shared by another. Often when one feels appreciated in this way, he can feel himself as capable of being loved; whereas when one feels depreciated or dehumanized, it is difficult for him to feel himself lovable to anything or anyone.

This being true, it is obvious that the chaplain must do far more than verbally proclaim God's love for it to be experienced. It is his task to help to foster a milieu in his own personal relationships (and hopefully within the hospital) where patients can feel that they are persons valued, important and loved. For when love is shared, God is already there.

But to help people experience God's love in this way is not the sole prerogative of the chaplain — it is every man's task. So the chaplain's task, or expertise, is common property. He would do well to remember this, as far as possible, to learn from and to help others to become more effective "ministers" to one another. One need not be ordained to bring into his relationships those qualities of sensitivity, concern, and faithfulness, qualities which enable and empower persons to more fully experience God's love.

This is not "a pastoral cop-out"; it merely reinforces the common priesthood and to summon all those in the hospital "to join a priesthood of the concerned." Perhaps the greatest danger confronting hospitals today is de-personalization. The massive, super-efficient, highly scientific and computerized system of medical care can be packaged and delivered in cellophane virtually untouched by human hands. To personalize this kind of bureaucracy is the supreme task of us all. If the hospital chaplain of today can mediate, mobilize and enable this to happen, then he has done his job well and God's love will have been experienced.

WORK WITH PATIENTS

Much of the chaplain's time is spent with the hospitalized patient. Broadly speaking, his task might be seen in this way: to help the patient retain his personhood apart from the devastation of his illness. It is easy for one to feel less than a person in an illness that strips one of strength, and body control and in a setting that deprives him of primacy and places him in a powerless, dependent situation.

Part of restoring personhood comes from listening sensitively to the patient. Little that a patient expresses in illness is irrelevant, but its deeper implications or intent may be missed by mechanical or insensitive listening.

Illness tends to bring life into sharper focus. It is a rich language which brings to consciousness one's attitudes, emotional involvements, values and commitments in life. A basic question is: what does this illness mean to this person?

Each person will respond to illness in his own way. That is his uniqueness. His response will depend, in part, upon the way he interprets his illness: Is it punishment for past sins? Is it the result of negligence? Is it a message of sorts from God? Is it an omen to mend his ways? Is it a prelude to death?

In an underdeveloped area such as Africa, individuals have many primitive ideas on the origin of illness. It is an evil spirit or a deceased ancestor retaliating or the result of a tribal law having been violated. A mother may be rationally convinced that a mosquito caused malaria in her child, but she is still left with the question, Why that mosquito and my child?

In a developed society, we are more sophisticated. Or are we? Many persons have equally "primitive notions" as to the origin of their illness. To listen for that, to respond to that person's interpretation of his illness and his feelings about it, is to take seriously his personhood.

The meaning of illness to an individual will also depend upon the ways in which he sees it interfering with his functioning. This will, in part, depend upon the emotional investments he has made in his body and his activities; it will also depend upon his values and meanings in life.

Will the illness interfere with important activities in the life of this patient?

Is it a threat to his capacity to love and to be loved?

Does it conflict with his need to be independent and productive?

Does it threaten his sexuality?

Does it distort the way he sees himself physically?

Does it alter his "patterns of adaptation," the habits he has developed to satisfy personal needs, maintain feelings of safety and reconcile his own needs with the demands of his environment?

These are the basic issues that a woman struggles with as she forfeits a breast or an uterus to surgery; or a business executive who has suffered a coronary; or an elderly person living alone who has sustained a broken hip; or an adolescent whose face has been scarred by a motorcyle accident; or a young mother whose baby has been born dead.

What does it all mean, now, to that person? To listen to "the voice of illness" and to enter into the anguish and questions of that person is a primary task of one who wants to minister.

Some patients may not know what it means. Others may express it in part, but unclearly. Others may express it clearly but without an awareness of its deeper implications. To sit and listen and wait and respond to these feelings and attitudes is to accord dignity to the patient, to say nothing of contributing to his self-awareness.

Along with listening, the chaplain helps one to retain his personhood by helping him to grow in the appreciation of his worth and resources as a person.

Illness can devastate one's sense of worth. It deprives one — even temporarily — of his role in society, it separates him from his clothes, work, play, family and friends, many of life's most important gifts. In a society which places such an enormous premium upon achievement, youth, vitality, hardiness, strength and efficiency, one can feel terribly useless as a sick person. The fact that family and job and friends carry on without him does not enhance one's sense of importance.

To represent God's love to a suffering person is most difficult. To help one feel his worth and resources as a person when he is physically and emotionally depleted, when he perceives himself to be unproductive and burdensome, is equally difficult.

Partly it comes from time spent with and interest shown toward the patient through sensitive listening. To focus upon one's feelings is to communicate that these are important. It is to communicate that though he is presently ill, and experiencing all of the limitations and confinements of that illness, he is still free to feel and to express those feelings. As these are important, so he is important. To feel listened to and responded to in this way is a rare and rich gift not often enough imparted and received. It could be termed, "human grace."

No doubt, to be verbally reminded that he is of God helps the patient to affirm his worth. To hear that God created him in His own image and has redeemed him through His Son, Jesus Christ, is to reinforce that one's value has never been in his work-a-day functioning which has now been sharply terminated by illness, but that it resides more deeply in his person.

Yet while God's love of man came prior to man's knowledge of it — or even before his existence — this love is most deeply and richly experienced when it is validated in human ways. God is not captured and limited to only those moments when His Word is spoken and His Sacraments administered. Where there is love, He is already there! When a patient experiences sensitive listening, authentic concern and warm affirmation — be it from a chaplain or a housekeeping aide — he has experienced God's love. Human love tends to sharpen and make more real the larger reality of God's love.

Sometimes the chaplain reaffirms the patient's worth and resources by "allowing" him to be responsible for his responses to his illness, as well as for his decisions. It is very easy for a chaplain (or anyone else in the hospital community) to become overwhelmed by the restrictive and destructive forces of illness and to fail to take seriously that person's capacity for responsible

[handwritten annotations: neurotic component → hostile-dependency Facilitate harmful adaptation to illness]

freedom. Perhaps to gratify one's own nurturant needs, or perhaps out of an overidentification with the patient's helplessness, it is tempting to feed another's dependency in a hospital. The whole strategy of healing tends to diminish a patient's initiative.

Part of that responsible freedom is to allow the patient to help determine the nature and goals of the chaplain's ministry to him. It is true that most chaplain-patient relationships are initiated by the chaplain. It is equally true that the most productive relationships occur when the patient senses a freedom on his part to define the nature of that relationship. It is often difficult for clergy to "allow" this kind of freedom.

But some patients want to be left alone, at least for a time; others may seek no overtly religious ministry; some want merely to engage in social conversations; others want only to have their hand touched, or their brow wiped; some want to seriously grapple with conflicts that have surfaced in the illness; some want to give, others to receive; some want prayer, while still others want to sit in silence.

Some may want pity, chiding, support, advice, scolding, reassurance or any combination of same. Some want something new and different, others want something familiar and traditional. Some are pleased the chaplain "doesn't really talk like a pastor," while others are disappointed when he doesn't.

Part of the task of the chaplain is to help patients articulate what they need and want in the relationship at this time. It is insensitive, to say nothing of rude, for a chaplain to continue to impose his needs upon every patient.

More often than not, the relationship will seek out its own depth and character, if the chaplain will allow the patient to exercise his responsible freedom.

It is important that the ill person be seen as an initiating, deciding person whose decisions make a difference. Even though many of his decisions may be limited to here-and-now hospital issues, it is important that they be exercised.

The chaplain helps to reinforce personal worth and resources when he enables the patient to respond creatively to his suffering. Viktor Frankl suggests that every situation in life contains potential for meaning and that the concrete task of every person is to relate his uniqueness to the pursuit of that meaning. He further states that even when one lacks the physical freedom to change his situation, he is nonetheless free to choose an attitude toward his experience. What Frankl seems to be saying is that frequently we have little control over what happens to us, but that we retain considerable influence over how we shall respond. To deal in the area of response, or attitude, and to summon one's capacity for growth despite physical limitations, is to reinforce one's responsible freedom.

When the chaplain has facilitated, mobilized and enabled the patient to deepen his self-understanding, self-acceptance and self-responsibility, he has contributed immeasurably to that person's well-being.

BETWEEN PATIENT AND PATIENT

The chaplain today is a mediator between patients. Hospitals traditionally have sought to isolate patients from one another. The physical floor plans reflect that approach, with the exception of psychiatric wards which have usually included day rooms where patients can play, eat and socialize. But on medical, surgical, orthopedic and obstetrical floors, little space is devoted to facilitate patient interaction. Consequently, hospitals have deprived themselves and their patients of a most significant source of healing: one's fellow-sufferers.

It is not that the patient lacks for people: physicians, nurses, aides, technicians, housekeepers, chaplains and others surround him. He is dependent upon them for services and he is not their equal. Besides, they are not sick. Patients need to reunite with persons who find themselves in a similar predicament, who face the same losses and deprivations.

At Lutheran General Hospital the chaplain has become "a mediator" between patients. He has helped to foster the idea of bringing patients together where dialog, empathy and mutuality can be a shared experience. This is done not only on the psychiatric floor (where group psychotherapy has been a treatment of choice for years) but on the coronary unit, the orthopedic ward, and the physical rehabilitation floor.

This is not to suggest that he has done it alone. He has joined forces with the physician, the social worker, the clinical psychologist, the nurse and others in stimulating patient interaction. This approach is not based simply on the premise that "misery loves company," or that "you'll feel better when you see someone who's worse off than you." While there may be some of this, patient groups provide a setting where feelings can be expressed, a sense of belonging can be experienced, coping methods can be learned and one can contribute to the lives of others.

The hospital community provides a patient's first social exposure while bearing the after-effects of his illness, whatever those may be. The kind of response he encounters through this social exposure, even though it be within the protective environment of the hospital, will deeply affect the way in which he sees and accepts himself. By providing realistic feedback to one another, patients can prepare one another for the reality each will face when he leaves the hospital.

To be a mediator between patients is an important task of the chaplain today.

CHAPLAIN AND STAFF

As has been said by many, too often the involvement of the church in the hospital is seen in terms of the chaplain. He becomes a symbol of the church's presence.

It is understandable, though superficial, to equate the church with the chaplain. It would rather seem that where hospital people are in touch with the agony of their fellow, there is the church, with or without the chaplain.

The chaplain today ought to be a mobilizer, an enabler and a legitimatizer of expressed human concern. It is not that he loves better or more deeply; but because of the symbolic nature of his role he can more readily validate human concern. People in a hospital often look to the chaplain as a symbol of compassion and honest concern. When he is these in fact, he helps many people; but he may unwittingly endorse the assumption that "the church is where the chaplain goes."

He may then miss his larger opportunity to mobilize "a

priesthood of the concerned." At his best, the chaplain is not in the hospital to do something no one else can (to speak to or for God) but to enable others to love and to care, and to help those same people see that this is what the Church and God and religion are all about.

The chaplain today contributes as best he can to the total healing milieu of the hospital. The time he spends with staff people — ministering and being ministered to — is as important as the time spent with patients. We have come to realize that what each of us does to another will profoundly affect what each does for the patient.

Consequently, the chaplain today has significant relationships with staff persons throughout the hospital. For in a hospital one is exposed dynamically to the struggles of man — struggles that are in all people. When they are graphically portrayed in a patient, they stimulate similar feelings in those of us who serve to that patient. To be a part of that struggle, to help others to deal with their human responses to suffering — as he is helped with his — is a rich experience for the chaplain. (For a more detailed discussion, see Chapter X, "Ministering to Staff.")

BETWEEN THE PATIENT AND THE OUTSIDE WORLD

The chaplain today is also a mediator between the patient and the larger community outside the hospital. Hospitals must continue to recognize that only a fraction of the healing occurs within its walls. Most of it takes place in the more familiar environment of the home and community.

To suddenly become a patient in the unfamiliar setting of the hospital can be frightening. Frequently the chaplain, though he is personally unfamiliar to the patient, represents something familiar to the patient. His presence often breeds trust and dispels some of the feeling of strangeness.

It is also true for families. They too may be puzzled and dismayed by the regimentation of the hospital and wonder if their loved one will be properly cared for. Again, because most families have had some familiarity with clergy outside the hospital, many find security in his presence, and he can play an important role in interpreting hospital routines to them.

Oftentimes staff become so preoccupied with meeting patient needs, that they have little energy or time for the concerns of the family. The chaplain can and does provide that concern and is a valuable link between the families and the staff. If families sense that their presence and needs are recognized, they become reassured that the presence and needs of their loved one will also be recognized.

He and others (such as the social worker) can be sensitive to the needs and responses this hospitalization has mobilized in family members. For they, too, are called upon to make significant adaptations and often with far less help than the hospitalized patient receives. At times this help may come in allowing feelings to be expressed; or it may be in offering reassurance; or helping to provide tangible services, i.e. transportation to and from the hospital, baby-sitting, meals for the children, by being a link with the hospital's volunteer group or with a local parish.

In short, illness is often accompanied by fears of rejection. The more significant people in the life of the patient that can be effectively mobilized to render concern, the less will be the feelings of alienation. The chaplain can be a key link between those interpersonal forces outside the hospital and the patient within the hospital.

Finally, the chaplain today can be a valuable link between the church and clinical research in the pastoral field. Granted much of the pastor's work is subjective and difficult to measure; yet there is a sense in which this has been used to hide his work from the scrutiny of research. The hospital setting with its emphasis upon testing and evaluating provides an excellent place for effective research. There are enormous questions that need to be raised about the force of religion in people's lives that can be clinically examined via sound research. It would seem that the church could learn much about its task and function by focusing in this area of research.

CONCLUSION

These are but some of the areas where the chaplain today

functions in a hospital. These areas will be explored in greater depth in this book by those who are spending their lives as hospital chaplains.

But this is the chaplain today: a *mediator*, a *mobilizer*, and an *enabler*, one whose basic vocation is to be among people.

II

THE INITIAL CALL

BRUCE M. HARTUNG

GRANGER WESTBERG calls it a "crucial" time (1); Arthur Travis calls it "an extremely difficult visit" (2); Charles Curran calls something like it a "brief encounter" (3). The "it" is the initial or random hospital call, made by a chaplain who enters a patient's room unsolicited by the patient. Here is the patient who enters the hospital for healing, who expects to be taken care of by medical and paramedical personnel. Here is the hospital chaplain, who thinks of himself as having an important part to play in the "healing team" in the hospital. He expects to make calls on the hospitalized patient in order that something or other might happen as a result of these calls.

The "something or other" may be the proclamation of the Word, as in Thurneysen, (4); or the establishment of an incarnation-like relationship, as in Wise (5). But this hospital chaplain has something to do or be with the patient; he enters the patient's room to do it.

The problem is that the initial hospital call presents a difficult situation. Numerous articles have attempted to deal with it by offering chaplains solutions to the pain of making the initial visit. Bruehl suggests that the chaplain needs to create a definite and limited relationship with the patient. This relationship needs to be communicated to the patient by means of a conscious structuring of the relationship. As part of the initial interview, Bruehl has the pastor say: "Yes, Mrs. Smith, I work with the Chaplain's office. You know I have no pills to give you, or tests to run, but I am interested in how you have been feeling about yourself through all of this, what it feels like to be you at this point in your life, if you would like to tell me. (The pastor here clarifies overtly and concretely why he has come to see this person (6).)"

In a similar vein, McHolland suggests that it is the responsibility

15

of the pastoral counselor "to define explicitly what the setting is that he is offering to *this* particular person who comes. That is, the counselor must know why he is present, what he intends to do and not do and what he expects of the counselee." For a hospital chaplain especially (since the relationship is initiated generally by the chaplain and not by the patient asking for a chaplain to call), the responsibility for delineating why and for what he has entered the room remains with the chaplain. The "why" and "for what" need to be communicated (not necessarily by words, McHolland would probably say) in the beginning of the relationship. He suggests that pastoral counselors need to learn to make clear what they offer to the patient. So also, to make explicit application to the hospital chaplain, the chaplain needs to learn to make clear what he offers (7).

Travis, also, recognizing that the patient has not requested a visit from the hospital chaplain, maintains that the relationship of the hospitalized patient with the hospital chaplain needs to be defined totally in the initial call. Travis points out that the patient "does not necessarily know from previous experience or from the context what rules are to govern their relationship." Since the hospital visit proceeds out of the autonomy of the chaplain, it cannot be assumed, according to Travis, that the purpose of this visit is at all understood by the patient. It is the responsibility of the chaplain to define the function of his visit.

Because the initial call is initiated by the chaplain and not by the patient, this call presents some problems to the hospital chaplain. Attempts have been made to remedy the problem, which behaviorally often takes the form of the reluctance of chaplains to make initial visits; and by presenting suggestions of ways to establish the contract with the patient so that both the chaplain and the patient have a clear idea of the "why" and "for what" the chaplain has entered the room. Such attempts to suggest means of contracting, while helpful, perhaps may be premature. What may be needed first is a serious look at the dynamics of the initial call to isolate the problem areas before solutions in the form of contract-setting are offered.

In a study conducted by the author, two selected nursing units at Lutheran General Hospital were chosen as wards with a special relationship to the Department of Pastoral Care (8). In the study the chaplains would make initial calls on all the patients but would not make any return calls unless specifically requested to return by the hospital patient himself. Behavior was measured, i.e. who called back for a hospital chaplain.

The chaplain made the initial calls and explained the procedure to be followed to call a hospital chaplain. Of the two hundred patients who were involved in this study, only ten called back for a chaplain. Of those ten, five called for Holy Communion. Only three called with specific "feeling" or emotional issues to discuss with the chaplain.

In follow-up interviews with randomly selected patients who did not call a chaplain, the patients were asked to imagine under what conditions they would call a chaplain. In all instances, when pressed, the patients stated that if they would call a chaplain, it would be in a time of serious illness when the prospect of death was imminent. Most did not call a chaplain during their recent hospitalization because they were not "sick enough," or "seriously ill enough."

Here is a situation involving a well-trained chaplain. His training has taught him to do theological reflection about his clinical experience. He probably has a reasonably intact theology in relationship to his patient calling in the hospital. His clinical training has taught him to respond to the feeling tones of the patient's communications and to be alert to the meaning of the patient's illness in the patient's own psychic world. The average trained hospital chaplain is relatively sophisticated both in his clinical expertise and in his own expectations of himself, both clinically and theologically. He has an idea of what he is about. That "idea of what he is about" is called his self-definition of his pastoral role.

Then there is a hospital patient, usually in the hospital for a brief time (the mean hospital stay in the study was 10 days). He has probably had some contact with a clergyman in his life, but that contact was most likely in relationship to the parish institution where most people see the clergyman functioning in terms of his highly visible roles, primarily in those functions relating to public worship and the maintenance of the institutional church (9, 10). Since the hospital chaplain is stripped of these highly visible functions, how then does the hospitalized patient see him? What does the hospitalized patient think the hospital chaplain is about? What the hospitalized patient thinks of the hospital chaplain is called the patient-definition of the chaplain's pastoral role.

ROLE DEFINED

In this study, the patient-definition was that the chaplain was good to have around when the sacraments were desired or when death was coming — when most all regular means of healing seemed to be failing. In addition, the chaplains were socially acceptable people who were good to have on the hospital staff. The patients in this research project did not decide whether or not to call a chaplain back on the basis of the chaplain's self-definition of his pastoral role; they decided to call or not to call a chaplain on the basis of their own definition of the role of the chaplain. That role was associated with bringing the sacrament of Holy Communion and of death and dying, when that role was associated with anything at all.

Thus the problem within the initial call may begin to be emerging. Role theorists teach that role conflict at one of many possible levels brings tension within the relationship (11). Whitley suggests that there may be ambiguity and conflict in the pastor's role as it relates to people, especially in the area of unclear role-definitions, the pastor's own self-image and his image of the ministry, and the pastor's understanding of his role and the cultural expectation of that role (12). The point is — and there may be many ways of conceptualizing it — that role conflict brings tension within the relationship. With the initial call of the hospital chaplain this research has shown that there is role conflict. The chaplain's own definition of his role is not identical nor is it really very close to the patient's definition of the chaplain's role. That brings tension.

How is that tension expressed? The chaplains who made the initial calls picked up little hostility. The chaplains said most people responded in at least an accepting, if not welcoming way.

In the follow-up interviews there was little indication that the patients were angry at the Department of Pastoral Care or any chaplain in particular. If the tension caused by the apparent role-conflict does not appear to be present with the patient, that only leaves one other place where it can be.

Tension does seem to appear on the chaplain's side of the relationship. It has been consistently difficult for hospital chaplains to make initial calls on hospitalized patients. (One of the most disliked assignments seems to be the "pre-op" call, which is basically an initial call on a patient the evening before the surgery procedure.) The policy of getting the initial calls made has needed repeating throughout the history of the Department of Pastoral Care at Lutheran General and probably in most pastoral care departments throughout the country. A consistent phrase used among the staff chaplains concerning chaplain students (especially one-year residents during their last quarter of training) is that they have difficulty "getting their bodies into the rooms." It is indeed difficult for the chaplains concerned to consistently make initial calls day after day in the hospital.

Another sign of this problem is highlighted by an informal survey taken at the conclusion of the research project. Clinical Pastoral Education supervisors at Lutheran General were asked if they ever concentrated on the initial visit in their supervision. All indicated that the vast majority of their supervision has to do with a continuing relationship established by the student-chaplain with a hospitalized patient. In other words, the student would bring in verbatim accounts of his calls on patients where a "relationship" had been established or where something "significant" had happened. In short, the chaplain-student would bring in verbatims where there had been some payoff in the relationship or where the differing role perceptions has implicitly been dealt with or had not been a problem. Rarely did the student bring in an initial interview, nor did the supervisor emphasize this as a suggestion.

As suggested by this research, the tension within the initial call is the meeting of differing role expectations or definitions with little attempt explicitly to solve the role-tension. If the hospital chaplain does not deal directly with the patient concerning the differing role-definitions, there is tension in the system which is shown most strongly on the part of the chaplain, who finds it increasingly difficult to initiate one more relationship which will probably be a source of unresolved tension to him. In some sense, the strain in the system (hospitalized patient-hospital chaplain) caused by differing role expectations might even be thought of as averse conditioning, which teaches the chaplain to avoid the area of pain — the hospital ward, specifically, patients on the ward.

An initial call is difficult because differing role expectations need to be hammered out within the relationship. The initial call will be even more difficult if the question of role expectations is allowed to remain under the table, implicit rather than explicit in the relationship. What is needed is either chaplains who are comfortable with what seems to be the overwhelming cultural expectation of what a chaplain does in the hospital (bringing Sacraments and comforting the dying) or chaplains who, in the first few minutes of an initial call, provide some kind of experience that makes explicit why the chaplain is in the room, if that "what" is different from the patient-defined role of the chaplain.

How this is done is the next step in a research program. Just as research is needed in therapy to determine what is effective — what helps people get better — so research is needed in pastoral counseling in the hospital to determine what methodology best communicates to the patient what the chaplain in the hospital is about.

There are various possibilities, each of which should be tested experimentally. These include the following:

1. The use of a brochure given to the patients, explicitly stating what chaplains are in the hospital for.

2. Utilizing a Curran-type understanding response, which gives the patient an experience of being understood without explicitly verbalizing the contract.

3. Following Bruehl's suggestion in which a chaplain may just come in and state, presumably in a caring way, what he is about.

All of these approaches may have good theoretical underpinnings, but research is necessary to document which of these approaches, or which other approaches, are more effective in dealing with the role-conflict and the resulting tensions.

REFERENCES

1. Westberg, Granger: The crucial first three minutes in the sick room. Pastoral Psychology, 16:45-47, 1965.
2. Travis, Arthur E., Jr.: Another look at the random pastoral hospital call. Pastoral Psychology, 22:46, 1971.
3. Curran, Charles A.: Religious Values in Counseling and Psychotherapy. New York, Sheed and Ward, 1969.
4. Thurneysen, Eduard: A Theology of Pastoral Care. Richmond, Virginia, John Knox Press, 1963.
5. Wise, Carroll A.: The Meaning of Pastoral Care. New York, Harper and Row, 1966.
6. Bruehl, Richard G.: Creating the pastoral setting. Pastoral Psychology, 21:26-34, 1970.
7. McHolland, James D.: Establishing the contract in pastoral counseling. The Journal of Pastoral Care, 23:36-39, 1969.
8. Hartung, Bruce M.: Requests of Hospitalized Patients for a Religious Ministry. Unpublished Ph.D dissertation, Northwestern University, 1971.
9. Fichter, Joseph H.: Priest and People. New York, Sheed and Ward, 1965.
10. Glock, Charles Y. and Roos, Philip: Parishioners' views of how ministers spend their time. Review of Religious Research, 2:170-175, 1961.
11. Ivery, Allen E. and Robin, Stanley: Role theory, role conflict, and counseling; A conceptual framework. Journal of Counseling Psychology, 13:29-37, 1968.
12. Whitley, Oliver R.: Religious Behavior: Where Sociology and Religion Meet. Englewood Cliffs, New Jersey, Prentice-Hall, 1964.

III

CRISIS CHAPLAINCY

RONALD LESLIE

"There's a DOA* in Emergency."
"Cardiac arrest on 7 Center."
"This is 6 East . . . we've just had an expiration."
"Pastor† they want you in Delivery."
"Mr. Johnson in Room 544 would like to talk to a pastor."
"Pastor, please come to the surgical lobby."
"I have an outside call for you, Pastor."

BEING, or even imagining that you are the hospital chaplain on the receiving end of any of these calls rapidly gives you the feel for crisis chaplaincy. You existentially become aware of its demands, its immediateness, its unknowns, its uncertainty and its stress. It tends to get the adrenal glands going and to make the armpits sweat.

Crisis chaplaincy is ministry to fellow human beings who are in the midst of experiencing an important, significant event — important because it is a life-changing, emotion-filled event in human history — for them. Crisis chaplaincy is ministering to the needs of these fellow human beings, being a pastor to them, communicating God's presence and love in situations that are infinite in number, kind, and intensity. This is a situational ministry. These are spontaneous calls for ministry over which the chaplain has little control and for which he cannot specifically plan or organize in advance. This is a ministry of brief encounters in the length of time spent and in the length of relationship. This is a nonstructured ministry; the chaplain has to play it by ear. This is ministry in a vast unknown — unknown facts, history, people, meaning, values and results.

Thus crisis chaplaincy is different from the regular floor

*Hospital life gives labels and abbreviations to many places and situations, e.g. *DOA* — *dead on arrival.*
†"Pastor" is the most common title used for chaplains at Lutheran General Hospital.

ministry in which the chaplain spends most of his time on a particular ward, is a daily member of the unit staff, sees patients on the unit regularly and perhaps several times during their hospital stay. It is different from counseling relationships which usually are longer, more leisurely and more in-depth. It is different from pastor-parishioner relationships which are of longer duration and which include a much greater degree of knowledge about the people, history and meanings that go into the relationship and ministry.

At Lutheran General, crisis chaplaincy is provided on a 24-hour, 7 days-a-week basis. There is a chaplain in the hospital and on call at all times. He is referred to as the "duty chaplain" and carries an electronic pager by which the hospital switchboard can transmit calls or messages immediately.

Calls for crisis chaplaincy may come from emergency, labor and delivery room, nursery, operating room, surgery lobby, or any hospital ward. The call may concern an expiration, a patient request, a staff member, or an outside phone call. It may be a preoperative call. It may be a chance encounter in the hallway with a patient, a nurse, a doctor or a relative.

"This is 6 East . . . we've just had an expiration. . . . " This seems to be the most common call for the duty chaplain. He is automatically called when a patient dies in the hospital.

Immediately he has several questions to answer and decisions to make. Is the family or any relative here? Do they know the patient has died? Who is the doctor? Will the doctor contact the family, or does the doctor want the chaplain to do it? Who of the family should first be contacted? If by phone, what should he do? These are the initial questions the chaplain is asking. He gets his answers and makes his decisions in talking with the nurses, the doctor and himself.

In a sense there may be some need for ministry to staff people and/or to doctors in an expiration situation. There may be a need for listening, for support, for forgiveness, for a sharing of guilt and grief. However, the primary ministry in an expiration is to the family of the patient. The chaplain meets them if they are there or when they come. He offers them (and may even encourage or push) the opportunity to go into the patient's room to see the body.

He goes with them and shares in their tears, their kissing and touching of the dead person, their facing the reality of death, their reluctance to let go and to leave, and he may do this without saying a word. He helps them gather the patient's personal belongings together to take with them as they leave. As they leave the loved one's body and room, the chaplain leads the family to a room where there is privacy and where they may sit together, cry together, talk together and experience their grief together.

The chaplain must decide how he can most helpfully minister to them – by silence, prayer, Scripture reading, touch, talk, questions? By communicating support, firmness, confrontation, approval, forgiveness? (At Lutheran General Hospital the chaplain has been delegated the responsibility of helping families in their decisions and signing of autopsy permits and of release papers to the undertaker. This becomes an additional part of his ministry with the family as they are sitting together.) With some families the need and question arises as to whether the chaplain should help them leave the hospital, or perhaps help them stay a little longer? Once the family leaves, the chaplain will probably never see them again. (At Lutheran General Hospital, the Department of Pastoral Care asks that he send a letter of sympathy to the family in behalf of the hospital.)

"There's a DOA in Emergency." This is also a common call and crisis situation for the duty chaplain. It is probably by nature the most traumatic in the sense of suddenness, intensity, unexpectedness and drama for all persons involved. It is one of the most anxiety-producing calls and situations for the chaplain.

As with an expiration, it is a death situation that calls occasionally for ministry to staff and always for primary ministry to families. The setting is the hospital's emergency room. The need is for ministry to intense and sudden grief. Most of the same questions, decisions, and functions described above in expiration situations occur in a dead-on-arrival situation.

Whether or not the family members view the body is sometimes dependent on its physical condition. Sometimes there is staff opposition and anxiety regarding family members seeing the body and perhaps disrupting the emergency room area. There is need in the emergency room area of the hospital for a room or private space in which the chaplain and staff can minister to families.

There are many other situations and calls for crisis chaplaincy to the emergency room: to talk with a psychiatric patient, a drunken woman, a child needing an emergency appendectomy, a husband and policeman whose wife has been accidentally shot by one of the children playing with his off-duty revolver. I recall sitting down with the husband-policeman. He felt confused and bewildered. His wife was three-months pregnant. No one knew for sure then how she had been shot. He went to a hospital phone and called home, only to find out that his 14-month-old boy had also been shot — apparently by the same bullet — and was taken to a different hospital. His father-in-law came. His wife was taken into surgery. He went to the Admitting Office to take care of admission information and papers. Then he left to go to the other hospital to find out how his son was. How to minister to this husband-father-policeman in this situation?

I sat with him for about 45 minutes while his wife was in the emergency room. I did not say much. I ministered by being with him and by sharing the feelings of "mess" and confusion. I did not know what to do or say and neither did he. I helped him find the Admitting Office, then said goodbye.

There is also a "waiting room ministry" in the emergency room context. If the chaplain has the courage, takes the initiative and makes use of his abilities to observe and perceive, he can go into the waiting room and find people who are in crisis and in need of companionship, friendship, support, comfort, a listening ear—a husband or wife whose spouse has had a heart attack; a parent whose child has a high fever. People sitting in the emergency room waiting-room, with a loved one somewhere behind a closed door, wondering what is happening to their loved one, call for a difficult yet meaningful crisis chaplaincy.

TYPES OF CRISIS

"Pastor, they want you in Delivery." So the duty chaplain goes to meet and be with a young couple whose first child has just been delivered stillborn. Or malformed. Or mongoloid. Or miscarried. Perhaps the obstetrician meets the chaplain as he comes to the labor and delivery area, and tells the pastor that Mary and her husband are in one of the labor rooms, that Mary has been in hard labor for several hours, that something is wrong and things do not look good. The chaplain and doctor go in together to talk with Mary and her husband. Perhaps a baby has been born sick, or a newborn in the nursery is now sick. The doctor or nurse calls to have the child baptized. The chaplain or doctor or nurse may have to tell the mother and father of the baby's condition; inquire about their beliefs, feelings and wishes regarding the child's baptism; baptize the child through the openings of an incubator; provide or arrange for follow-up pastoral care to the parents in the days following. The labor, delivery, nursery and maternity units are often the setting of crisis chaplaincy.

"Pastor, please come to the surgical lobby." At Lutheran General Hospital there is a special lobby area for the families, relatives, and friends of surgical patients. Here they anxiously sit and wait while their loved ones are in the operating and recovery rooms. Here the doctor will meet them when the operation is over to inform them of its success or failure and of the condition of the patient. Here the chaplain can find much need for ministry.

He can sit with families and help them share and express their common feelings of fear, sadness, worry and hope together. He can offer the support of prayer. He may serve as a communication link between the operating and recovery rooms and families. If a family is getting more and more anxious because surgery is lasting longer than they anticipated, the chaplain can go into the operating room area, obtain general information from the nurse regarding the patient's condition and how much longer the surgery will last, and communicate this back to the family.

A surgeon may have bad postoperative news for a family. Sometimes he asks the chaplain to accompany him into the lobby to talk with and inform the family. As in the emergency room waiting area, the surgical lobby calls for creative ministry to families in crises.

Working in Surgery

Occasionally, there is a need for the chaplain in the operating room itself. One chaplain received such a call from the surgical nurse, stating that a woman had "panicked" on the operating table just before being put to sleep and had refused to go on with the operation until she saw a clergyman. The chaplain was gowned and masked before entering the operating room where he joined the patient, five nurses, the surgeon, and the anesthesiologist. His conversation with the patient went as follows:

Chaplain: "Can you hear me?"
Patient: "Yes, I can hear you."
Chaplain: "You wanted to see a clergyman before going to sleep?"
Patient: "Yes, I haven't been baptized."
Chaplain: "Would you like to be baptized?"
Patient: "Yes."
   The anesthesiologist tells the chaplain the patient's name, a nurse gets a bowl of water.
Chaplain: "You can't recognize me because of the mask, but I am the chaplain who visited you in your room yesterday afternoon."
Patient: "Oh, I don't know if I talked enough then?"
Chaplain: "We had a real good talk. Would you like to be baptized now?"
Patient: "Yes."
   The chaplain performed the baptism.
Patient: "Thank you."
Chaplain: "Thank you. You can relax now, relax and go to sleep, it's all right."*

In this operating-room crisis the chaplain provided a ministry of support and comfort needed by the patient, and did so by means of sacramental ministry. It was a ministry needed for the total care of the patient.

"Pre-op" Visits

Preoperative or "Pre-ops" is an important area of crisis chaplaincy. Preoperative or pre-surgical pastoral visits are made each evening to patients who are scheduled for surgery the next day. This is a difficult kind of ministry. The chaplain has to enter into several new and brief relationships repeatedly. He meets the

*Rev. Merton S. Fish, a 1970-71 CPE resident at LGH. Information and quotations from a written verbatim done by Chaplain Fish.

psychological dynamic of denial constantly. His own expectations and idealism regarding a "good" pastoral visit are challenged and shattered over and over. His own need and definition of "helping" is often frustrated. Yet sometimes he feels involved in a creative, comforting and giving ministry.

He may facilitate a patient's sharing and expression of pre-surgical fear and loneliness. He may pray with the patient. He may give the Sacrament or he may read Scripture. He may give verbal encouragement, support and hope. He may do any of these with the patient individually, with the patient and his roommate, or with the patient and family members who are present.

"Mr. Johnson in Room 544 would like to talk to a pastor." The chaplain may receive such a patient request for a pastoral visit at any time of the day or night and for almost any reason. The chaplain goes to the patient unsure of the need, the situation, what he will do or the results. It may turn out that the patient just needed someone to talk to about rather superficial things, or about specific and personal concerns, that he wanted prayer and the Sacrament or that the patient was a manipulative psychiatric patient.

"I have an outside call for you, Pastor." And the chaplain finds himself talking on the telephone with an intoxicated woman, a person wanting marriage counseling, a father worried about his depressed son or a relative inquiring about an expired patient. One of the slow, hard lessons the chaplain learns is that the primary ministry often needed (or the crisis chaplaincy called for) is a ministry to the caller rather than to the person the caller is calling about. Instead of coming up with solutions and arrangements, satisfying the caller's outward request, and hanging up the phone ("You can take your depressed son to the Family Counseling Service.") the chaplain focuses on ministering to the deeper and more subtle needs of the caller on the phone.

"Hallway ministry" in the hospital is even more subtle and spontaneous than the telephone call. The sensitive chaplain may find himself ministering to (listening, encouraging, confronting or accepting) hospital staff and patients in the halls, the chapel, the cafeteria, the doctor's lounge, the library, the snack shop, or even the parking lot. These are the "bumping into" encounters which may be quite casual and brief, yet very meaningful for the chaplain's role and for the hospital community. This too, is a part of crisis chaplaincy.

A Classic Example

In describing the many areas of crisis chaplaincy and what it is like, I want to share a single experience in my own crisis chaplaincy. I call it "My Valentine, 1970."

It was February 14, 1970. I was on night duty. Around 8:15 P.M. I wandered out to the lobby area to see if any people were waiting around. In the surgical lobby there was a girl about eight years old. She was sitting at a table doing her school work. There were also two women sitting together across the lobby area.

I walked over to the girl, introduced myself and struck up a conversation and found out her name was Janet. She was doing her homework.

"We're waiting," she said, "my father is upstairs in the Intensive Care Unit."

"Oh . . . is he visiting someone or is he a patient?"

"No, he's a patient."

"Is that your mother sitting over there?"

"No, my mother is dead."

Having put my feet in my mouth already, and being "stunned" by Janet's information, I ended our conversation and stumbled over to the two women who were sitting in the lobby.

I introduced myself, asked if they were related to Janet, and found out one was Janet's aunt and the other was a neighbor. At this point all three of us noticed Janet was sitting and crying quietly at her table. Her aunt said to me, "She's afraid the same thing is going to happen to her father that happened to her mother. Her mother died five years ago today on Valentine's Day. Janet hasn't seen her father for several days."

My heart was beginning to ache for this little girl. The pastoral wheels began to spin in my head. It was now around 8:30 P.M. It was dark outside and getting quiet in the hospital. Visiting hours were over and people were gone. Children are not allowed to visit in the Intensive Care Unit, but Janet needed to see her father!

I went to ICU. I talked with the head nurse and described what had just happened downstairs in the lobby. Her heart agreed with mine. The two of us went over to Janet's father. We checked with him to see how he was feeling and what his condition was.

"Mr. R., Janet's downstairs in the lobby. Would you like to see her?" "Yes." And his eyes lit up. Together the nurse and I shaved his three-day-old beard. I went downstairs and talked with Janet's aunt.

"Do you think Janet would like to see her dad? Could she take it?" "Yes, I think so." We went over to Janet. "Janet, would you like to go upstairs and see your dad?" "Yes."

We went to ICU. The nurse and I showed her to her father's bed with the curtain pulled around it for privacy. We left the two of them alone together for about five minutes. Then the head nurse and I joined them. The nurse was crying and tears were in my eyes. The nurse aide was sitting at her desk crying. Janet's aunt and neighbor joined Janet and her father.

After about a 20-minute visit, Janet, her aunt, the neighbor lady and I went downstairs. We said goodbye. They went home. A Valentine had been given. A ministry had been done. There were many hearts in it. Many had ministered and been ministered to — including me.

ISSUES AND SKILLS

There are at least four general areas of *issues* and *skills* involved in crisis chaplaincy. What are the issues? And what skills does it take for the chaplain to meet them?

First is the issue of *the unknowns* and *anxiety* of crisis chaplaincy. This issue has been pointed to and alluded to from the beginning of this chapter. It refers to the necessity of the chaplain entering into situations and relationships faced with a vast number of "unknowns" and to the resulting and natural anxiety he feels in the face of these unknowns.

When he receives the message or call, he does not know all the facts of the situation; the people involved; their feelings, thoughts, fears, hopes, needs or values. Perhaps he does not know their religious affiliation or denomination. Finally he does not know what he should or would do to minister in the situation.

The skill needed to initially meet these unknowns and anxiety is a personal skill. The crisis chaplain must have developed an awareness and knowledge of himself as a person. He must be aware of how he reacts to stress and anxiety and what abilities and strengths he has to put to use. He must be able to perceive his own feeling responses to events and to people, and be able to incorporate them into his action-decisions.

It takes skills of personal maturity, courage, initiation, and openness to situations to enter into the unknowns of crisis chaplaincy. Thus the chaplain's training and development is a process of personal-professional growth and development. In clinical pastoral education programs, the student chaplain focuses his experience, observation, reflection and evaluation on himself both as a person and as a chaplain.

A second issue is *perception of need — ministry done.* What does the situation call for? What is needed? Who needs what? In crisis chaplaincy there must be an accurate perception of the need for ministry before the chaplain can attempt to serve those needs. Does the patient need to talk? Or to act? Or to be left alone? Does he need comfort or confrontation? People's needs and situations for ministry vary greatly.

Thus the crisis chaplain needs skill in diagnosis and in decision-making. He must be a flexible diagnostician and minister. He must know and believe that religious needs, values, and meanings can and should be served and shared in different ways at different times with different people. At times he may function in a passive, silent-presence role; at other times he may function in an aggressive, assertive, directive role.

A third issue is that of *group ministry.* Quite often the crisis chaplain finds himself attempting to minister to a group, usually the family of the critical patient. Or sometimes he enters a patient's room expecting to make an individual pastoral visit and finds visitors and relatives in the room. Then what? Does he say hello and goodbye and promise to come back later? Or does he perceive an opportunity for "group ministry?"

Along with the growing use and apparent effectiveness of small groups in the educational and therapeutic fields today, some of the most meaningful and effective ministry can be done with a group of people rather than individually, e.g. how about "group pre-op visits?"

A nurse could gather the six or eight pre-surgical patients on her unit together, along with any family members who are present, and the chaplain could spend 10 to 15 minutes with this group of people, facilitating some degree of sharing and discussion of preoperative feelings and fears. Hopefully, patients and families would experience a sense of common identity and community, and would continue to minister to each other long after the chaplain was gone.

In order to do group ministry, the crisis chaplain needs skill, knowledge and experience in group process and dynamics. His CPE peer-group experience and training is a vital part of his education for group ministry. Other group training and experience such as sensitivity groups, encounter groups and therapy groups are also helpful. But the crisis chaplain also needs an "intangible" kind of skill for group ministry – he needs a theology of community, a belief in the Body of Christ, as the foundation for his group ministry.

A final issue is that of "Results, Effectiveness, Value, Worth and Helpfulness." Was I helpful? Did I do a good job? Was it worthwhile? Perhaps the most difficult thing about genuine ministry is its lack of "seeing results." The crisis chaplain may never know how he has helped someone. Or whether what he did was effective and helpful. Thus he needs the big skills of faith, belief, trust, and hope in God, in himself, in "togetherness in Christ," in the uniqueness and worth of relationship between human beings. He needs these in order to be able to give of himself, briefly and unknowingly.

CONCLUSION

In crisis chaplaincy, the basic need and goal is ministry to the fear and loneliness of fellow human beings. The crisis chaplain ministers by communicating and sharing God's presence in and through himself. He is involved in adventures in faith. His basic belief and trust is that God works in strange and mysterious ways.

IV

MINISTERING TO THE
SURGICAL PATIENT

ARTHUR J. REE

"AND a little child shall lead them." This Scriptural
truth has served the author in good stead in his ministry to the
surgical patient. Still remembered is the day when a seven-year-old
taught his father a lesson which provided an insight into learned
comfort in expressing fear, a lesson which has helped considerably
in aiding the surgical patient to recognize, accept and healthily
deal with his fear of anticipated surgery.

The child, second of three sons, had been ill with a sore throat
which did not seem to be getting much better. The family doctor
was out of town and, on this particular day, so was his associate. It
was necessary to take the boy, Kirby, to a doctor whom the boy
did not know. After father and son had checked into the doctor's
office, they were placed in an examining room. The boy climbed
up and sat on the examining table. His father sat in the chair.
Together they waited for the doctor. Kirby was quieter than usual,
and the father wondered what he might be thinking, so asked,
"Are you scared?" The frontal, direct approach was a little too
strong and may have conveyed some kind of impending judgment,
for the boy quickly answered, "No!" The father tried again: "You
know, Kirby, there have been times when I've been in a strange
place with strange people, not knowing what was going to happen,
and I was scared."

The boy listened without comment. About three long, heavy
minutes went by and then he said, "Daddy." The father asked
"What?" And he answered, "I'm scared!"

The lesson was a pointed one: that one cannot deal with his
own fear by trying to talk himself out of it, nor can one ever help
anyone else deal with his fear by trying to point out all the reasons

33

why he should not be afraid. Letting Kirby know that it was all right to be afraid enabled him to accept it in himself, and, in the process, be somewhat less afraid. Needless to say, the father's response was to take his son in his arms and let him know that he would be with him through whatever might come.

There have been many instances since that day when the insight gained was applied beneficially in a ministry to the patient anticipating surgery, or the postoperative patient. Perhaps one of the most dramatic of such instances, and one which delineated the need for such a ministry, came on the day the author was called to intensive care to visit a patient about to undergo emergency surgery. It was a critical situation, cardiac surgery on a patient with a diagnosis of dissecting aortic aneurysm.

The surgeon had already spoken to both the patient and his family before the chaplain was called. After speaking briefly to the patient's wife, and learning of the seriousness of the procedure and the fact that its seriousness had been communicated to the patient, the chaplain entered intensive care. Necessary preoperative procedures were underway. During a lull in the activity, the chaplain approached the patient and introduced himself. The patient, with a look of gratitude, said, "I'm so glad you came, Chaplain. I know I may not get through this thing, and I want to make my peace with God."

He went on to describe how his life had not been particularly devout, in terms of membership in a church or attendance at worship services, but that he knew of and appreciated the love of God. As patient and chaplain talked, with an emphasis on the patient's fear of the impending ordeal and the chaplain's open acceptance of the fear, a perceptible change came over the patient's countenance and he began physically to relax.

He made his confession, of both sin and faith, and finally said, "I'm ready. Now I would like to talk to my family."

The risks were great enough for the surgeon to have told the family that the patient might not even survive the initial incision. The patient sensed this. He had some unfinished business to take care of, one item of which was a desired reconciliation with an estranged son. Having been able to deal with his fear, and through prayer, having made his peace with God, he was now ready to attempt the other important reconciliation, with his son. The chaplain brought the family in and then left them alone. When the son came out the chaplain went back in to the patient, who said, "Chaplain, I'm ready now for whatever might come."

There is an aftermath of the story which supports the thesis that having been allowed and even encouraged to talk about his fear, the patient did not have to carry that extra burden into surgery. Some months after his heart surgery, the patient's wife became a patient in the same hospital. In the course of visiting her, the author had occasion to renew his acquaintanceship with the patient who shared with the chaplain how during the conversation that took place immediately before surgery, he had been terrified. He had felt the fear draining away and being replaced with confidence, trust and a realistic acceptance of whatever might happen.

It was an experience which the patient remembered during the long, painful and frightening postoperative convalescence, and from which he continued to derive confidence and emotional strength. His was certainly not a "death-bed conversion," but because of it, he was able to restructure his value system, and to some extent, life style. He was profoundly grateful to have met someone who allowed him to talk about that which truly bothered him, without feeling the need to minimize or discount the feelings.

A ministry had been offered, and was accepted by the patient. That helped him set things in proper perspective through the process of being where the patient was and hearing him out without being prematurely supportive or reinforcing any denial which might have been present.

CRISIS MINISTRY

The surgical patient provides an opportunity for the chaplain to deal with people in crisis. A surgical in-service instructor often says to beginning chaplains in clinical pastoral education, "From a patient's point of view, there is no such thing as 'minor' surgery. It's all very significant to the patient."

A patient checking into a hospital for surgery, whether it is elective or emergency, finds himself in crisis. It is crisis with three major components:

1. It is pin-pointed in time, being relatively immediate.

2. It is identifiable, because the surgeon has discussed with the patient in the office or in the hospital room the procedure that is going to be done.

3. It is anticipated, so that some preparation has already been done in terms of business and family affairs, which will ease the mind of the patient during his absence from home and work.

The crisis begins when a patient sees her family doctor about a lump she has discovered in her breast, and he says, "We'll have to check that out. I'll bring in Dr. X, a very fine surgeon I know."

Or it begins when another patient decides it is about time he has something done about that hernia which has been plaguing him for years, and his doctor says, "We can get you an appointment for surgery for two weeks from Wednesday."

Or it begins when, with a rending crash of cold Detroit steel against the even colder concrete bridge abutment, the patient finds himself with a compound fracture of the left femur, necessitating open reduction.

The time is pinpointed, whether it be a month from now, two weeks from now, or even yet tonight. It is known by the patient that at the particular time appointed by the circumstances, he will have to submit to being put to sleep and having things done to him while in that state that, in spite of the level of present-day lay knowledge of medicine, still remains somewhat mysterious. The chaplain is able to explore with the patient, and such exploration is facilitated by the time element, the meaning of this experience to the patient, and to offer the support, encouragement and understanding as the need indicates.

The fact that the crisis of surgery is anticipated in no way minimizes or alleviates the concern that might follow. The anticipation might even generate greater anxiety and apprehension because of the inexorable march of time. As the hands on the clock continue their journey around the face, the thought very often seems to present, "I'll be going in twelve hours . . . in eight hours . . . in two hours . . . any minute now," and there appears to be a corresponding increase in the level of anxiety.

On the other hand, the waiting period before the surgery might be viewed in terms of, "I wish they'd get at it and get it over with." This feeling seems to be engendered by the idea that the average layman has that the surgical procedure is the crisis, and the crisis will be over when the procedure is completed and he is awake from the anesthetic. The fear of the patient centers on the anticipation of what is going to happen and when it is going to take place. The fear of the surgeon, on the other hand, seems to center not only on the procedure itself, but on the possible postoperative complications, a fear which the average layman undergoing surgery scarcely realizes. The physician is on guard until the critical, immediate postoperative period is over, and being "on guard" means an alertness to complications that could be fatal.

The crisis of surgery is also an identifiable crisis because the patient is usually quite aware of what needs to be done and why. The ability to identify the crisis as such (when surgery has been scheduled and is therefore anticipated) is also related to the possible unknowns. The woman who is scheduled to have a breast biopsy is never really sure whether or not the pathologist's finding will be positive or negative and based on that finding, she may or may not have to undergo a radical mastectomy before she leaves the operating room.

The chaplain ministers preoperatively in helping the patient face up to the worst possible consequence of her surgery and to help her deal realistically with those feelings. The crisis of surgery, while being identifiable, is also a crisis simply because all elements, all factors, all variables and all possible consequences are not readily identifiable. This fact makes the surgery a crisis, which is where the chaplain can focus his ministry and help the patient to find meaning for even this experience in her life.

PATIENTS NOT IN NEED OF MINISTRY

It is obvious to the chaplain as he makes his pre-surgical visits, that not all patients are in need of his ministry. Many do not have unmanageable apprehension. Many patients will admit to the presence of some "nervousness," but tend to dismiss its significance with a kind of *que sera, sera* attitude. Other patients will exhibit a great deal of fear, apprehension and concern, and be more than ready to talk about it and look for some alleviation of it.

A factor that seems less of a predictive factor than might be suspected in determining which patients are most likely to be apprehensive is that of "seriousness" of the surgery. Any two patients with the same provisional diagnosis, and scheduled for the same surgical procedure, could easily display entirely different attitudinal postures. One might easily be taking the whole thing in his stride while the other could be "climbing the walls." The same thing about predictive factors could be said regarding the frequency of surgery for any one particular patient. It is not a predictive factor in determining the presence or absence of apprehension. It is erroneous to assume that the more often a patient has to undergo surgery, the better able he will be to handle his fear and apprehension. One might also assume, again erroneously, that the patient will remember such things as postoperative pain and misery and be more fearful with each succeeding surgical procedure. Neither assumption is necessarily true. It happens both ways.

The author remembers the feelings he experienced as he anticipated his first two back surgeries, and the apprehension was not at all unmanageable in either instance. The third time he was scheduled for the same operation, his anxiety was almost overwhelming. This illustration supports the thesis that it is not always true that each succeeding surgery will be more easily managed emotionally. On the other hand, the author has visited patients who were having repeat surgery, and found attitudes of, "I've been through this already, and it's not so bad." This supports the thesis that it is not always true that each succeeding surgery will be more difficult to handle emotionally because of the memory of postoperative pain and misery.

It is a truism that each surgery case has to be considered individually. Frequency of surgery or "seriousness" of the procedure cannot offer any kind of prediction of what the chaplain will meet when he enters the patient's room. The 18-year-old, scheduled for a tonsillectomy, can be more frightened about it than a 45-year-old having his third cystoscopy and transurethral resection.

MANY FEELINGS OF THE PATIENT

We have spent a great deal of time talking about fear and apprehension in the surgical patient, but there are other feelings in the patient to which the chaplain must minister. A change in body image, through the results of surgery, can have deep psychological and spiritual implications for the patient. The amputee patient will have questions about the return to relatively normal functioning and whether or not he will be able to accomplish that return minus his arm or leg. The whole question of worth and value as an individual will merit some astute ministry by the chaplain.

The "great American syndrome" dictates that an individual's "productivity" is threatened by an amputation, or by cardiac surgery which necessitates the adoption of a new style of life, and so he feels that he has lost his worth. The chaplain's task is to convey to the individual in a way that is reassuring, that his worth is based much more on his "being" than on his "doing." The "being," the existing, of an individual always precedes his "doing." It is "who he is" rather than "what he does" that makes of an individual a valuable person. More particularly, who he is in relationship to himself, to other people and to God enables a person to affirm his own worth.

Body image is a factor that also comes into play in terms of sexual identity. For example, the woman with a mastectomy or a hysterectomy will have questions regarding the lessening or feared loss of her femininity. The man who has to undergo an orchiectomy because of carcinoma will experience some of the same kind of feelings regarding lessening or loss of his masculinity. Generally, there are many forms that the anxiety of the surgical patient will take, and the chaplain ought to be aware of some of them. Anxiety over body image is only one.

FINANCIAL FEARS

There may also be some anxiety over the financial situation of the family, which may be under some threat because of the breadwinner's hospitalization and surgery. In some cases, this anxiety will supersede the anxiety over the actual surgery — the implications of the surgery may have more to do with the patient's anxiety than the surgery itself.

What all of this means to the surgical patient and to the chaplain who ministers to him is related to the patient's view of life. The patient's relationship to God has a direct bearing on his attitude toward his experience of surgery. The author often meets patients whose feelings about illness and surgery seem to be focused on the "will of God." What is looked for when this attitude is present is whether it is destructive of, or expressive of, faith.

Not wanting to impose upon the patient his own theology, the chaplain will not take away from the patient that which is supportive of his faith. If the patient says, "It's the will of God," and does not seem to be particularly perturbed that God should treat him this way, this chaplain will not be anxious to correct what he feels is erroneous in theology, or doctrinally unsound. If on the other hand the patient asks, "Why does God treat me this way?" the ministry to that patient is clear, and takes the form of putting suffering in its proper perspective, namely, that God does not will suffering, but He does will for us meaning in it.

Chaplains at Lutheran General Hospital provide surgical patients with a preoperative visit. He is open to a discussion of whatever the patient feels the need to discuss. Very often the visit is focused on the immediate concerns of the patient regarding his forthcoming surgery — the fears, the apprehension, the questions about the present and future implications of the surgery.

Many times, the visit is simply the expression of concern and interest, and the chaplain does not push the patient to talk about things he does not want to talk about. The patient who expresses gratitude for the pre-surgical visit, in which very little was talked about in reference to the surgery, is saying to the chaplain that he is appreciative of the concern and interest even though he chose not to discuss his feelings about his surgery. The patient who takes advantage of the chaplain's visit to do some thinking out loud about the immediate and long-range future as it relates to his surgery, also expresses appreciation for the visit and the opportunity to look at some things about his own life and his present feelings. Both patients illustrate the way in which a chaplain's visit might be used. The ministry is offered, and it is left up to the patient whether or not he will accept it.

Such a ministry is also offered to the families of surgical patients who spend their time during the surgery of their family member waiting in the surgery lounge. The chaplain will check on the progress of the surgery, or on the patient's stay in the recovery room and make such progress reports to the family.

Hopefully, the patient's own anxiety is dealt with in the pre-surgical visit. The chaplain ministers to the family in their anxiety while they await the surgeon's report. Both of these kinds of ministry expect cooperation between the surgery floor nursing staff, the recovery room staff and the surgeons.

The chaplain enhances such cooperation whenever he chooses not to become a medical expert, even though a knowledge of some surgical procedures can facilitate his ministry. His concern is the patient, and the patient's family, and not the exhibition of medical expertise. He must remember that he is concerned about the total person, but he does not apply himself too vigorously to the assimilation of knowledge of surgical procedures, except as such knowledge can contribute something in the way of understanding to the patient's situation.

There are many things that could have been said about ministry to the surgical patient, but those things are not unique to this kind of ministry. The psychodynamics of illness prevail with the surgical, as well as the medical, patient. The feelings of threat to existence, of loneliness, dependency and loss of self-esteem through a change in body image, are all present in some degree or other during the crisis of illness and hospitalization, and no less so with the surgery patient. The chaplain will do well to remember in his ministry to the surgical patient, the importance of meeting each patient as a person, being sensitive to the individual, and the sometimes unique way in which each person handles the crises in his life. An unstructured way of indicating to the surgical patient that barring any unforeseen complications, all will be well, is to say and be serious in intention, "I'll see you tomorrow."

V

MINISTERING TO CORONARY
PATIENTS AND THEIR FAMILIES

ARTHUR O. BICKEL

As part of a nationwide study of the rehabilitation of patients with cardiovascular disease, a group of renowned cardiologists including Paul Dudley White sent questionnaires to forty general practitioners. One question was: "In the order of their importance, what measures have you found of value in the rehabilitation of your cardiac patients?" The following response came as a surprise to many clergymen:

> Consultation with persons in related fields and use of ancillary agencies was reported by the general practitioners surveyed to be of limited value. In many areas in which these doctors practice, such facilities are entirely lacking. Ministers were reported to have been the main source of extra-medical help to the general practitioners and it was noted that when the patient had the advantage of faith, ministers were of particular value (1).

The report is not explicit about the specific contributions made by the ministers, but their assistance must have been of significant value for the physicians to mention it in answer to the open-ended question. Just as parish pastors can be useful to general practitioners, so too can hospital chaplains contribute significantly to the healing of heart attack patients by participating in group meetings with other health care professionals and patients.

A program of group meetings with patients has been in effect at Lutheran General Hospital since the late 1960's and has met with enthusiastic support from physicians, patients, their families and medical personnel. In this chapter, the goals and methods of these meetings, the experiences of the patients and specific opportunities for pastoral care will be presented.

GROUP MEETINGS

The idea for group meetings came from patients. They

42

expressed their individual concerns and sentiments to physicians, nurses, dietitians, chaplains and social workers. It was apparent that though there were personnel in the hospital highly skilled in many fields, no single person on the staff had enough knowledge, skill or time to assist all the patients individually with their concerns. Patients expressed concern about their conditions, their prognoses, their work, their diet, their families, their finances, their values and goals, and a variety of other facets of their lives which were being affected by having experienced a "heart attack." Expressions such as these were heard:

"I don't think I'm as sick as they think I am; I sure don't feel sick."

"How am I supposed to take it easy with a wife and three kids?"

"They say I have to change jobs. But that's easy to say and hard to do when you're 50."

"The food around here makes me angry; it's got no taste."

"I can't be an invalid the rest of my life."

"There's going to be some changes made in my life."

The initial motivation for starting the group meetings was twofold. First to make more economic use of time in serving patients. One hour spent with one patient could be the equivalent of six hours if we were meeting with six patients in a group for an hour. Second, the hospital is committed to an ecological concept of medical care which in this setting means, in the words of the Rev. Fredric Norstad, one of the founders of Lutheran General Hospital, "we accept responsibility for treating persons rather than simply diseases." (2)

Didactic-Therapeutic Sessions

The conceptual model has been a combination of didactic and therapeutic. About one-third of the time is planned for didactic material and about two-thirds for therapeutic. The word therapeutic here is used in a broad, less intense sense than would be indicated by the word psychotherapeutic. The therapeutic aspect of the group process involves personal issues, concern on the part of the leaders, not only for the information the patient is picking up, but what he is doing with the information or what it is doing to him.

Goals and Format

The goals are basically these:

1. To supply relevant information.
2. To encourage patients to verbalize their questions and their feelings primarily with reference to their heart attacks.
3. To facilitate the patients' support of one another.
4. To give patients opportunities to help themselves.
5. To serve more patients in the available time.

Groups meet each week day for an hour each afternoon in a conference room on the floor which has the largest number of coronary patients. The group averages about four patients with two or three relatives present. It is a continuing cyclic format so patients can enter the group or leave on any day they are ready.

On Monday the didactic emphasis is on anatomy — what happens when a heart attack occurs, how the doctor diagnoses it, how the heart heals ideally. This material is presented by a nurse.

On Tuesday, a dietitian discusses the various types of diets and when they are used. Wednesday, a nurse presents general health guidelines dealing with the issues of gradual increase in activity, continuing out-patient contact with physician, occupation of idle time for several weeks, medications and possible recurring pain.

Thursday, a chaplain presents material on the relationship of stress and heart attacks, identifying the feeling of stress, its origins particularly with reference to life goals and values, ways of expressing the feelings of stress and suggestions for keeping stress within moderate bounds.

Friday, a social worker has the option of presenting either material on communication, family relationships, returning to the job, attitudes of society or using the hour with a kind of "you teach us" theme. Then patients are asked, in effect, to share what it is like to have a heart attack and what they experience in the course of their recuperation.

Patients who attend the group are in the latter phase of their hospitalization when they are allowed to sit up for an hour each day. The physician's consent is a prerequisite for attendance. Relatives are strongly encouraged to attend and participate in the group. There are usually two or three present at each meeting.

In order to maintain a degree of continuity in the group, two leaders are present every day, a hospital social worker and a chaplain. Besides providing continuity, they encourage and precipitate group interaction and personal focus.

MEDICAL CONSULTATION

A staff internist meets regularly with the coronary group staff serving as a medical consultant and as a liaison between the program and the medical staff. He is appointed by the medical director of the hospital. A physician is not present in the meetings for two reasons:

1. It is felt that a physician may find himself in a delicate position between the patient and the patient's personal physician.
2. It is anticipated that the physician might tend to shift the focus of the group simply by reason of his professional position from group interaction to a one-one relationship between individual patients and himself.

EXPERIENCE OF PATIENTS

Significant results have occurred both for the staff and for the patients. For the staff the results center about the fact that there is better understanding of the uniqueness of the person who has had a heart attack.

Here are some unique facets seen. Abrupt onset of the disease is common. Many heart patients have had no warning. They have had no opportunity to adjust to the prospect of being hospitalized or of contemplating the significance of their disease in their lives. As a consequence, their adjustment begins with hospitalization.

Society has taught people to accept some responsibility for the occurrence of a heart attack. With most other diseases such as cancer, appendicitis, gallbladder disease, respiratory problems and nerve disorders, the average patient is apt to feel he is a victim of a organ malfunction or a disease intrusion and has in no significant sense contributed to his disease. The heart patient, on the other hand, is much more inclined to ask the question, "What am I doing wrong that caused this?" It is found that heart patients are generally motivated to inquire, to learn, to change and to accept responsibility for avoiding a recurrence of a heart attack.

The painful symptoms are often of short duration. It is not unusual, after a day or two in the coronary care unit, for the heart patient to experience only sporadic pain or no more pain at all. Patients often express dismay at how good they feel and how severely they are restricted. Initial symptoms were often vague or diffuse and seemed disassociated from the heart. Indigestion, perspiration, pain in the arms, pain across the shoulders and general fatigue leave the patient confused about what might be causing the distress.

Both the short duration and diffusion of symptoms tend to support the denial mechanism which, it has been observed, is the most common means which heart patients use to cope with the implications of their problems, particularly in the first days subsequent to the attack. In the group at some appropriate time, patients are asked if they think they've had a heart attack. It is surprising how many still hope, even after they have been hospitalized as long as three weeks, that their symptoms are caused by some other problem. A typical patient still relying on denial as a coping mechanism will say something like, "I didn't have the real symptoms. I had some indigestion but very little pain. I've had trouble with my stomach for years. I seriously wonder if it wasn't just some of the old stomach disturbance."

Myocardial infarction, the medical term for a heart attack, involves an organ crucial for continued life. The threat for the patient with heart disease is much greater, therefore, than it would be with a disease affecting a less crucial part of the body. Patients are able to relax their denial as a means of coping with this serious threat to their existence when they are helped to find other options for coping, such as a realistic hope of return to an active life and acceptance of moderate limitations.

Patients are seldom able to look at or to express for any length of time the concern about the possibility of their sudden death. They do talk around it in group and may touch on it directly for a bit, but then shift the topic to other matters.

A final unique phenomenon with heart patients is that they

suddenly experience the loss of the most basic human prerogatives such as feeding themselves, deciding when to get in and out of bed, where and when to defecate and urinate. If grief is defined in a broad sense as the reaction to loss, the loss of the heart patient is substantial and, therefore, the immediate grief is ample. This creates an unusual amount of frustration, anger and anxiety.

It seems that grief, the experience of loss, is more common and more often encountered by the heart patient than fear. Also, the implications of all that has been lost is what most patients struggle with in adjusting.

It has been observed that there are four clusters of adjustment behavior which occur most commonly: denial, dependency, depression and realistic adaptation. (Ministry to patients will be discussed in terms of these four clusters in the last section of this chapter.)

RESPONSE OF PATIENTS TO MEETINGS

The response of the patients has been consistently and emphatically positive. The criticisms they offer have to do primarily with time allotments and keeping the lecture content at a comprehensible level.

The didactic content is appreciated by those who attend the group because most patients acknowledge ignorance about their condition. It is a relief to them to become informed. Physicians question the possibility that some patients at this stage of their recuperation may be more harmed than helped by the information offered. In view of the patients' response, this concern seems unfounded. Whatever problems the information may create, they appear to be minor compared to the benefit to the patient. Dynamically, the presentation of information tends to dispel much of the unknown which tends to reduce their anxiety. They express appreciation for the information which helps them to understand what has happened, where they are presently, and what lies ahead of them. The information is quite general and almost elementary. Still the patients appreciate it deeply which is indicative of common ignorance about heart attacks.

Patients appreciate the group discussions. Both in written evaluations and verbally they describe their reactions in words such as, "It made me feel less alone." "I felt a common bond." "It's good to hear that others have the same problems." "I felt the concern of the rest of the group." "They helped me with some of my questions." "My problems seemed easier and smaller when I heard about the problems of others." "I felt I helped others and that was a help to me." "It made me realize that we are all unique in some ways yet similar in others." "The questions of other group members helped fill me in." "This was a chance for me to release some of my apprehensions."

At times some patients are irritated by other patients. However, even these patients felt they had received benefits. Their feeling was that they could have benefited more if one or two patients had not been there. When one considers that people in crises tend to use each other for help in everyday life, it should be no surprise that they received help from each other when given the opportunity in a hospital. The privacy of single and double rooms in modern hospitals has some distinct disadvantages.

In examining and categorizing patient responses on written evaluations requested of them, several therapeutic dynamics occur.

1. Patients feel a sense of acceptance from each other. This may be appreciated more than usual because their disease has created many problems for themselves, their families and their work, which tends to make them feel like they have quickly become more of a liability than an asset.

2. Patients find that expression of their concern, fear and apprehension is beneficial in itself and is accepted by others. Ventilation is therapeutic.

3. One of the surprising dynamics mentioned by patients is that they felt a renewed appreciation for their own uniqueness. It may be that hospitalization tends to minimize the individual identity of patients and that it is renewing for them to be in a group meeting setting where their unique identity is reasserted and recognized by the group and staff. This is a frequent and emphatic response in evaluations.

4. Mention is made of the benefit they receive from what might best be described as observation of others. They gain from

listening to and observing fellow patients.

5. A considerable number of patients appreciate the feeling of being "in the same boat" with other people. This kind of response seems to be more than an appreciation for some kind of passive support. It has an element of active assertion, as if they have become part of a select "in-group."

6. One of the consistent sentiments expressed is appreciation for the interest and help of the staff. An underlying message which they are receiving from the staff is that we care enough about them to make the effort to meet in groups and offer our services. Perhaps this is simply an awareness that we are trying to do more than is usually done.

7. A final benefit appears to be that patients are offered an opportunity and setting to test the soundness of personal and popular attitudes and information about their heart, which they have picked up in their lifetime from a variety of more or less reliable sources.

OPPORTUNITIES FOR PASTORAL CARE

Patients respond to the experience of a heart attack with essentially two emotions, both of which are of immediate concern to the chaplain: The first, most commonly expected, is fear of death. However, it is our experience that it is more commonly experienced by patients. This has been observed repeatedly by medical personnel working closely with heart attack patients.

The grief experienced by patients centers in a variety of losses, real or imagined: the loss of strength, of virility, of ability to work, or earning power, of usefulness to their family and of capacity to engage in pleasant activities or hobbies. It is not unusual for a heart attack patient to picture his future life as a gloomy existence for having lost too much.

Denial

Characteristically patients react to the fear and grief by denying, becoming dependent or depressed or by realistic adaptation.

If the patient denies, he is apt to invoke comments like, "No, I never dreamed of having a heart attack. I never thought I had anything like that." Patients are apt to blame their symptoms on almost anything besides their heart.

Another form of denial is the expectation that in a few days everything will be as it was. Denial is the most dangerous of all adjustment if it continues for long, because the patient will do little or nothing to help himself and after discharge will not cooperate with a recovery program.

Denial can be very frustrating for those who are trying to help. However, it may be helpful to realize that denial, within limits of time and intensity, can be a gift of God. It affords the patient a chance to gather his energies and resources to meet the crisis.

When extensive denial persists beyond a week or two, the problem of assisting the patient to be more realistic (a vital religious concern) becomes a delicate one. Of course, blunt confrontation with reality is neither wise nor merciful. The chaplain is challenged to walk a path between overburdening the patient beyond his powers and understimulating him to do the adjustment work necessary.

Sometimes it is appropriate to raise the issue, if the patient avoids it, by gently asking something like, "Joe, you know I've been to see you several times, and I've been wondering what this experience means for you and your family." Almost always patients respond to that kind of frank encounter, particularly if he has come to trust that the chaplain will not be judgmental or give unwanted advice.

If the denial persists and the patient has a parish pastor, it might be advisable to contact the pastor and urge that he help the patient get in contact with the Heart Association for informative, helpful materials. (The biography of President Eisenhower is frank and encouraging for heart patients.*)

Religious convictions and behavior may be used both to help with denial but also to support inappropriate denial. Comments such as "I'm going to trust the Lord and He'll see me through. I'm

*Dwight D. Eisenhower: *The White House Years, Vol I: Mandate for Change, 1953-1956.* Garden City, New York, Doubleday and Company, 1963.

not going to think about it," may or may not be expressions of mature, healthy religion. Christianity encourages eventual facing of reality. It is in the presence of life as it is that faith has the most meaning. The chaplain will do well to assess considerately but critically the nature of individual religion and help the person to more realistic and mature religion if the patient needs it and is capable of it.

Dependence

Dependent reactions have two possible directions, either to lean on others for guidance, advice and support or to blame others for inadequate guidance and support. In effect what patients who respond in this way are saying is, "I've got a problem and someone else caused it and/or I'm leaving the solution to someone else."

Typically a patient will say he is leaving everything to the doctors and nurses to decide. This is a very helpful and essential attitude for a while, but eventually the patient is obliged to assume some responsibility for recovery or it will be impeded. If the dependent reaction continues too long, it ends in a state which has been called "cardiac invalidism."

The chaplain's role is important with such patients. The patient has anxiously moved into a world with new demands, admonitions and cautions. It is not too different from a child's experience as he grows and develops except "the child" here is an adult. A generous, considerate response on the part of the chaplain is needed, coupled with respect for the patient's adult status and dignity as he is helped back to a more independent life. If the family has leaned heavily on a father or mother, members of the family may have to do some major adjusting when that father or mother cannot be leaned on. A vital ministry to the families may be in order.

The chaplain may serve temporarily as a substitute father or mother. He may represent to the patient a comforting, supporting and protecting God both in work and deed. Creative listening is vital as patient and family pour out their appreciation or frustration. Some attempts to talk about the crisis are vital if only to confirm a wait-and-see attitude.

Questions concerning the will of God are sometimes raised by heart patients. Leslie Weatherhead has offered necessary clarification in this matter.

"Man should part forever with the idea that sickness or disease is the inscrutable will of God and that resignation is the attitude of mind required of us . . . God's primary will is perfect health." (3)

Sometimes the secondary will of God is a concept used to describe the fact that sin, sickness and death have entered God's creation and that He allows it to enter our lives while promising to bring good, even out of disease. But healing and health are the ends for which God's people, pastor and patient, depend on God while they work toward those ends themselves.

Depression

The depressive reaction of patients is typified by attitudes and moods of discouragement, sadness, anger, frustration or guilt. With the majority of patients depressive reactions are temporary.

The chaplain can help the depression to be temporary if he accepts with understanding. At the heart of depression, anger is usually present and some of that anger is felt toward God. It is important for the chaplain to distinguish between the anger of love and the anger of disinterest.

The anger of love, of confused or disappointed trust, or of frustrated hope requires acceptance by the chaplain. The anger of careless disinterest will be more appropriately met with confrontation. The patient is apt to be angry with anyone and everyone: family members, God, hospital staff or himself.

Dynamically, depression is thought to be anger turned inward. It is common among heart patients because society has taught that people have more responsibility and control over a heart attack than over most other diseases. The patient thus is often inclined to blame himself, to ask, "What did I do wrong?" Though there may be no evident answers, it is important for the patient to express the feeling behind the question. For experiencing and living through painful feelings is an indispensable part of healing.

Adaptation

Adaptation involves a process of surrender (not compliance or resignation) to the reality of heart attack and of effort to fit or conform in whatever ways necessary. It often involves a reassessment of life's values and goals to see whether they are healthy.

Ideally, the clergyman is *the* professional person to help the patient think about his life style and his values. The chaplain, who has taken the time to establish a relationship of frankness and trust with the patient, need not be shy in raising such issues. A typical conversation might proceed as follows.

> *Chaplain:* "I've been wondering, George, what all of this has meant to your life and what you live for."
> *Patient:* "I've done a lot of thinking lying here. I've got a feeling I'm going to make some changes."
> *Chaplain:* "Changes?"
> *Patient:* "Well, I worked long hours getting my business off the ground. Trouble is, I got it off the ground all right, but I went right on working night and day. It isn't necessary now. I don't even know why I did it. At first I had to, but not now."
> *Chaplain:* "You got it rolling and let it carry you with it."
> *Patient:* "Exactly." (pause) "My wife has almost raised the kids by herself. She asked me often to spend more time at home, but I felt like I had to work to keep things going. We've talked together since I came here. I'm going to be spending more time with my family, enjoying them, helping them to grow up."
> *Chaplain:* "That sounds like a wise decision to me. And it may be good for your heart too. Do you think you'll be content spending more time at home?"
> *Patient:* "I think so. This whole business has made me do some thinking about life. I have a feeling God wants me to help my wife and kids more and enjoy them. I'm going to try it. You know, I figure if I work as hard at that as I did at the business, it's bound to work."

Alteration of values and goals is a difficult adjustment to make. It is easier to leave them intact and find new ways to achieve them. So the clergyman has a challenging task in helping patients examine and alter values.

Two simple but profound concepts of the Christian faith are vital for the heart patient and the chaplain is in a position to help a patient discover or reaffirm them. They center around the good news of the New Testament. One is *grace.* The patient who knows deeply the acceptance of God with all limitations, faults and inadequacies, is less apt to push himself beyond reasonable physical and emotional limits. The other concept is the central theme of the Christian ethic, namely *love*. The patient who decides he is going to spend more time with his family may be reaffirming the giving and receiving of love as a valid goal for life.

Having a heart attack is a profound experience in mortal existence. The patient is blessed if he is ministered to by a clergyman who embodies a measure of the love and wisdom of God.

REFERENCES

1. Williams, Bryan, *et al:* Cardiac rehabilitation — Questionnaire survey of general practitioners. Journal of the American Medical Association, 165:791-794, 1957.
2. Norstad, F. M.: The Lutheran Institute of Human Ecology. Lutheran Social Welfare. 9, 1:39, 1969.
3. Weatherhead, Leslie: Psychology Religion and Healing. Nashville, Abingdon-Cokebury Press, 1951.

VI

PASTORAL CARE FOR PATIENTS IN A PHYSICAL MEDICINE AND REHABILITATION UNIT

ARMAND NORDGREN

MUSCULAR dystrophy, Parkinsonism, cardiovascular accident (stroke), multiple sclerosis, cerebral palsy, brain damage, arthritis, spinal cord injury, amputations — these are some of the diagnostic terminologies applied to the people who are admitted to a hospital's physical medicine and rehabilitation unit for treatment and care. For such patients, and for their families, their affliction is usually severe and tragic. Their stay on the unit will be relatively long and the upgrading of their remaining potential function usually will be stressed rather than the actual cure of their illnesses or injuries. Their adjustment to their handicaps will depend partially upon their own inner strengths and partly upon the help and support of many concerned people, their physicians, families, and friends, the unit staff, and community resources.

In the hope to offer patients maximum rehabilitation in several areas — physical, social, emotional, vocational, economic, recreational and spiritual — a number of skilled people representing a variety of professions work together as a team. This is both desirable and mandatory.

This chapter will describe in part the history of one patient of the hospital's rehabilitation unit and the chaplain's role both with this patient and in relationship with some of the other members of the rehabilitation team.

Joe (not his real name) was a 42-year-old assistant foreman employed by a construction firm. He was involved in a serious accident at work. He had fallen from a scaffold and was taken by ambulance to a nearby hospital where it was determined that he had suffered multiple fractures, some internal injuries, and brain damage the extent of which could not be initially determined. He underwent emergency surgery at that hospital and remained there for intensive care during the first few critical days. Upon regaining limited consciousness and after the most immediate physical crisis, during which his life hung in the balance, had somewhat subsided, he was transferred to our hospital because of its physical medicine and rehabilitation unit.

THE REHABILITATION-UNIT CONCEPT

The rehabilitation section functions on the concept of human ecology. Its staff is committed to caring for a patient as a whole person in relation to his environment. The staff attempts to assist him in redeveloping and maintaining the physical, intellectual, emotional, social, vocational and spiritual aspects of his life to the extent that he has need of these. In a simplified but broad sense the unit's goal is to help restore its patients to their maximum potential.

The attending physician maintained medical management of Joe while he was a patient in the unit and received close cooperation from the members of the rehabilitation team. The team is directed by a physiatrist (a specialist in physical medicine) and includes a rehabilitation nurse, a physical therapist, an occupational therapist, a speech pathologist, a psychologist, a chaplain, a social worker, a recreational therapist, a clinical nutritionist, a vocational counselor and an administrative person. Some of the staff have either co-workers or assistants in their respective professions. Most, including the chaplain, give all or most of their time and effort to the unit and its patients.

One cannot describe the specifics of the roles which each member of the team developed with Joe while he was a patient, except to say that each had a significant part in Joe's rehabilitative process. Most have long worked together in a common effort with patients. Through in-service meetings each had presented what he considered his own unique task would be with patients in relation to the other disciplines which the team represented. Group meetings, "feeling" sessions and retreats had been held by the staff and had helped considerably toward achieving mutual understanding, commitment and loyalty to one another.

Staff Communication

Since communication among the staff is considered to be of vital importance, there are several means by which this is achieved. Each week staffing meetings, grand rounds, clinics, program planning sessions, and in-depth conferences are held. Relatives often attend when requested. The staff is expected to participate actively in all of these.

Members of the team have the responsibility of communicating with the attending physician and with each other verbally and on the patient's chart. The chaplain, for instance, describes briefly, on the "ecology sheet" of the chart, his ministry to the patient. Together with his co-workers he submits a weekly written evaluation on the "progress sheet." Since he is on the unit almost daily, he is in close personal touch with both patients and staff. The climate regarding communication is a healthy one. The chaplain feels that he would find it difficult to function as a "loner" or in a vacuum even if he wanted to do so (which of course he does not).

The chaplain learned about Joe's admission by attending an initial staffing at which Joe and his condition were described. Brain damage had caused some degree of aphasia (a loss of communication which is more than just loss of speech). Joe's aphasic condition was recognized to be both receptive and expressive in that receptively his ability to understand the spoken and written word was impaired, and expressively he encountered difficulty in gesturing appropriately and in speaking and writing as he used to do before his accident.

The staff was aware in the early days of Joe's hospitalization of his bizaare speech and inaccurate and inappropriate use of language including vulgar words and phrases but accepted these without amusement or anger. The speech pathologist, who took a key part in patiently retraining Joe to communicate, reminded the staff that language functions which are lost through aphasia sometimes return in the order of their original development.

Meanwhile Joe's struggle with relearning the art of communication seemed to the chaplain and others to parallel the bewilderment, frustrations, anger and depression which tormented him in his trauma.

Joe was able to relate to the chaplain soon after he was initially hospitalized. In the beginning, the relationship was limited because of Joe's acute physical condition. For a time the chaplain's visits were brief but frequent. Perhaps it was the clerical collar the chaplain was wearing which first prompted Joe to say, "Hello, Father." It was not until several weeks later that Joe, a Roman Catholic, learned that the chaplain was a Protestant clergyman. By that time it did not seem to matter except to amuse him.

"Anyway, you're the same as a priest," he once said. The chaplain never bothered to dwell on the difference with Joe lest it add to his confusion.

Progress Reported

The greeting which Joe gave the chaplain was noted on the progress sheet and at a staff conference. It was considered to be a mark of progress in his reorientation as to time and place and distinguishing of people. Later Joe identified the speech pathologist, the chaplain, the physiatrist, and some of the nursing staff. As Joe began to know the chaplain better, he also seemed to want to trust him. His wife had told the staff that "he always felt an obligation to the church and respected the clergy." An assumption was tentatively made therefore that through Joe's former contacts with the priests before his accident, he had the opinion and possibly feeling that the clergy usually can or should be trusted. The chaplain attempted to encourage Joe's trust.

For a while it seemed that the chaplain was among the few whom Joe did trust. Once when he was very belligerent, needed to be restrained and medically tranquilized, the nurse on duty requested assistance of the chaplain, who tried to interpret the procedure. He informed Joe that the medicine would help. Joe eventually consented to receiving a "hypo" saying to the chaplain,

"O.K. if you say so. The nurse can give me the shot, but not you." The trust seemed to be strained, but not broken.

On the other occasions Joe refused physical therapy treatments claiming that they were too painful. Hearing of this, the chaplain offered to go to a therapy session with Joe, who consented to the arrangement. The time spent in therapy was brief, but the therapy was not cancelled.

Joe's dependence upon the chaplain seemed to grow because of a trusting relationship which had developed between the two. Later his dependence subsided as his reorientation developed. Slowly he was able to relate better to a growing number of the staff whose care was important to him, not the least of whom was the physical therapist. Meanwhile the rehabilitation team encouraged Joe's independence and self-reliance (where therapeutically indicated) as one of his goals in the integration process. One of the pitfalls that a staff may encounter in caring for long-term patients is to foster, quite unwittingly at times, an over-dependence that is not really required. But good team work is an asset in preventing it, since usually someone on the staff recognizes the tendency and can point it out as he sees it happening.

Since complete cure is not usually in the picture for the permanently disabled person, there are some reactions to his problem that he needs to work through. Joe, for instance, was often depressed and to some degree expressed feelings of guilt. He tended to blame himself for the accident which caused his injury, stating often enough that he should have been more careful.

Intertwined with his depression were feelings of anger which were directed both inwardly at himself and outwardly at family, staff and other patients. He talked proudly of the responsibility he had assumed in his employment, then angrily detailed how hard he had to work to keep up to get the jobs done and that he felt compelled to perform tasks that those under him could not do as well as he. He expressed resentment at having had to do "risky work."

Nearly all of the staff became aware of his depression and often felt his anger. The chaplain was no exception, "Leave me alone," Joe said, "You bother me just like the rest of them." Few patients with permanent disabilities escape feelings of depression, guilt and anger. An experienced staff member should be able to recognize these emotions and to assist the patient in understanding and dealing with them.

A final word about Joe. After several months he was discharged from the unit. Thereupon he was regularly scheduled for out-patient speech, vocational and physical therapies for several more weeks. He has his ups and downs and finds it hard to be the husband and father that he formerly was.

He is employed again, not at his old job as an assistant foreman, but he is working regularly. On one of his out-patient visits he seemed to sum things up in stating, "My mind is still scrambled, but not as much as before. You all helped me, but God must have had a part in my comeback too." The chaplain and probably most of his co-workers on the rehabilitation floor are willing to accept that.

Other Factors

Ignoring or failing to accept a disability is another reaction with which a patient may need assistance. One young stroke victim discarded the sling for his paralyzed arm whenever he could. In doing so he seemed to be denying the paralysis. Perhaps later he may recognize and accept his handicap, but until he does so all attempts to help him develop and improve his remaining physical resources stand in jeopardy.

Another patient was often observed frantically rubbing the paralytic hand hoping unrealistically for a return of feeling and function. Since the chaplain seemed to have a fairly good relationship with him, he could in his concern and with some confidence ask, "Do you sometimes wonder if the hand will ever come back?" The question led to a serious and realistic discussion which in turn seemed to prompt the beginning of the person's acceptance of his handicap. Now he is better motivated, with the capable assistance of the occupational therapist, toward developing more competent function of his "good hand."

The rehabilitation team considers the use of groups to be of high therapeutic value in the restoration of patients to their maximum potential. How groups are used will not be discussed in this chapter, but it should be stressed that handicapped people can be helpful to one another in the group process. Often there are several ongoing groups on the unit at any one time. Group methods are applied by several of the staff, two examples being the occupational therapist using group techniques to achieve better results in a dressing program and the speech pathologist doing the same with expressively aphasic stroke patients.

The chaplain has often worked together in patient groups with social workers, nurses, and the psychologist. Though not purposely structured toward a religious emphasis, questions are often initiated, pondered and worked through by handicapped persons in group — questions such as, "Have I been so bad to have had this handicap?" "Why has God allowed this to happen?" "What am I worth now?" "Is life worth living anymore?" These are basically religious issues and serious attempts to achieve solutions to them are important.

Families of severely handicapped patients often have heavy burdens to bear and should not be forgotten. For this reason they are invited to attend weekly group meetings. Here the chaplain is involved as a co-leader with one or more of the rehabilitation team, i.e. a social worker, nurse, clinical nutritionist, speech pathologist, occupational and physical therapists.

The use of prayer, the presentation of appropriate scriptures and the offering of the Sacrament of Holy Communion are resources traditionally unique to his ministry which the other helping professions leave untouched. The chaplain has not discarded them but uses them especially when requested and when in his judgment he feels this emphasis may be helpful.

Participation at the hospital's Sunday religious services, the Protestant worship and the Catholic mass are encouraged for rehabilitation patients. Off the unit privileges, whether to the lobby, cafeteria, gift shop or outside grounds, are stressed and since "chapel" is included in this category the staff is geared to transport patients via wheelchairs, carts, or assisting them to walk to the chapel.

This chapter is not meant to be an all-inclusive discussion of the role a chaplain can take in a rehabilitation situation. Rather, it should be viewed as how one particular chaplain functions in one particular setting.

Not all patients are like Joe. Not all patients relate well to the chaplain. Yet, functioning as a part of the rehabilitative team, it is the chaplain's hope that he too can make a contribution to the restorative process which the staff attempts to bring to each patient.

VII

EMOTIONS AND ILLNESS

HAROLD S. NASHEIM

A SCIENTIST recently said that greater developments have been made in the areas of transportation and
communication in a single lifetime than in all the preceding
centuries of human history. The flight of the Kitty Hawk to the
moon-landing of Apollo XIII and the voice of Bell on the simple
telephone to live lunar television transmission are among the
obvious examples. Since these receive widespread publicity, we
tend to lose sight of some of the equally significant though less
dramatic developments taking place in the world.

Since World War II, great advancements have been made in
medicine. Within our lifetimes we have experienced great strides in
the treatment of disease, the alleviation of suffering and the
extension of the average human life span. But the celebration of
these accomplishments has been drowned out by the clamor for
greater benefits to greater numbers. New chemical substances are
discovered, new modes of surgery are developed, and new forms of
radiological and physical therapies have been developed to lessen,
if not eradicate, suffering and pain and human misery.

CHANGING CONCEPTS OF ILLNESS

Out of such fantastic development with subsequent benefit has
come specialization and diversification of both knowledge and
treatment. Though no one can be oblivious to the blessings that
have resulted, neither can one ignore the questions and concerns
that it has also produced. What is illness, disease? Such a question
gives rise to others, such as, What is pain? or Who has pain? Not
only where is the disease, but also who has the disease? Not *what*
is ill, but *who* is ill, for the *organ* cannot be treated as an unrelated

63

part of the person, but rather the *person* must be treated who possesses the physical organ that is calling attention to the disease. Paul Tournier in *The Meaning of Persons,* says, "Moreover the need to specialize accords priority of the organ over the organism, turning medicine into a brilliant technique, automatized down to the last detail" (1).

This approach to the whole subject of illness and its treatment is not so much new as it is a reclamation of a basic truth — that it is the person who is ill, not simply a body. If it is just the body that is ill, then it becomes diseased only in relationship to its individual parts or organs. It is then a self-contained, independently functioning unit, not affected by or affecting any other unit or person.

If it is the person who is ill, then his illness must be considered in the light of his relationships with other persons. We often speak of a "sick" society or community, a "sick" educational, political, or religious system. These are not indiscriminate, undefinable masses; these are persons living, functioning in relationship to one another. The person cannot live a self-contained existence, independent of any other.

Rather than specializing only in the body system and its functioning during illness, perhaps there is need also to specialize and explore the person system and its functioning during illness. This would seem to be one of the great developments in the area of illness and its treatment in the past couple of decades. As a result there has been opening up a new interdisciplinary approach to the study of illness and the treatment of the person. To be sure, this does not minimize whatsoever the great breakthroughs and continued exploration in scientific, physical medicine. But it readily recognizes that it is the person who is ill, the person not merely as a body, but in his relationships with his self and with others. This person, often unable to function in a satisfying, fulfilling manner becomes ill, is diseased. To treat only his body without concern for his other relationships, social and spiritual, is to be concerned with only part of the person and bypass other areas that can be basically significant in his illness. Psychosomatic medicine has recognized the effect of psychological concerns upon the body system and introduced another dimension beyond the physiological. But its very name designates its limitations to the psyche and the soma of the person.

In this time of change, with its dynamic evolution in the field of human health care needs, the opportunity is given to participate in what is being recognized as the spiritual, as well as social needs and relationships of the person who becomes ill.

FACTORS THAT CONTRIBUTE TO ILLNESS

The laboratories of the physical sciences have for a long time supplied evidences for the cause of illness to the human body. Out of the same laboratories have come formulae for chemical substances with which to treat the causes. Now with the broader concept of the illness of the whole person comes new opportunities for research and development of both causes and treatment yet to be developed.

The factors that contribute to the illness of the person seem to be as various and numerous as the persons themselves. These factors and their development are too complex to allow for simple categorizing of persons and illnesses into neat little groupings and indexes. Much more research and study must continue in the phychological, social, emotional and spiritual dimensions of the personality, in order to move from the general to specific evidences of the relationship of emotions to illness.

Patterns of evidence are beginning to evolve, however, in the ecological program of treatment on the medical units of our hospital. There remains little doubt that emotional stress and frustration are basic contributing factors to many physical illnesses. Such a concept is not readily accepted, particularly by the person with a medically diagnosed illness. There seems to be little difficulty in accepting the fact that such stress contributed to psychiatrically diagnosed conditions as depression, anxiety neurosis, etc. Peter Fletcher, in *Understanding Your Emotional Problems*, describes it well:

> Our emotional life is so obviously related to our mental activity that most people recognize the value of psychological treatment for disturbances like inferiority complexes, phobias, and anxiety states. It is less easy to believe that our physical illnesses can be directly caused

by anything as substantial as an idea. To many people the suggestion that a bodily disorder of any kind whatever can be relieved, let alone cured, by a change of mind, sounds manifestly absurd.(2).

Many individuals in great physical distress will readily accept the medical diagnosis of stomach ulcers, ulcerative colitis, or asthma. But they will forthrightly reject any suggestion that possible emotional stress in their lives is contributing to, if not causing the distress. Like sin and human weakness, it is much more readily recognized in another than in one's self. Patients have been known to find it very understandable that someone else's problems and difficulties in life can affect their physical health, but fail to recognize how "mine, which are so little in comparison, have anything to do with my sickness."

Mrs. A. complained of much dizziness and frequent headaches. She had no difficulty in accepting the medical diagnosis of high blood pressure and to submit to medical treatment. She traced the onset of her symptoms to a seige of the flu which she had several months earlier. Her husband had died about a year earlier but she felt this had nothing to do with it, as she considered his death a blessing, releasing him from an incurable illness with long-extended suffering.

She had gone to work soon after his death and had been busy with many activities, so she did not believe that there was any question of unresolved grief. However, what she failed to reckon with was the emptiness and the loneliness which she experienced when she was confined to her apartment during her flu episode. She had been needed while her husband struggled with his illness; now unable to work for a period and being isolated, she felt unneeded and considered herself unwanted. It was impossible for her to be aware of or to deal effectively and constructively with her feelings.

The case of Mrs. A. illustrates not only the relationship of her emotional stress to her physical illness, but also one of the main reasons why it is so difficult to recognize the relationship. She considered it wrong on her part to grieve, for this would be selfish. She could only say how fortunate it was for her husband to be freed from his suffering but refused to allow herself to openly grieve or to share her tears with anyone, including her children who were adults and willing to share her sorrow and expressions of loneliness.

For many patients, all negative feelings are to be denied and rejected as wrong. This is particularly true of feelings of anger or hostility. Early in the formative years, they have been taught that to have angry feelings is sinful and such angry feelings will bring eventual punishment. The justification for such repression of anger usually runs like this: "Anger is a bad feeling; if I am angry I am then a bad person; such badness makes me unacceptable, rejected by myself, others and God."

Oftentime it is possible to recognize anger, to admit to it to others, but not appropriately to the person or situation which causes the angry feeling. The usual response is, "Oh, I would only hurt them if I expressed it to them." When asked who is now being hurt, such persons frequently admit, "I am."

Mrs. P. was forced to flee from her homeland with her family because of the persecution by the dictatorial powers that ruled there. She had seen many of her close relatives suddenly removed from their homes and killed. She described her childhood home and family as one in which there "was much Christian love," and in her youth and adult years she had participated in many evangelistic meetings. She could describe in detail the years of terror and fear under which they lived. When asked her feelings about the dictator and his ruling clique, she would say, "But I must not be angry with them, that would be wrong." She could speak of the anger of God toward those who had been so cruel and that God would bring His judgment upon them, but she denied having any anger of her own. She sought help for her frequently recurring chest pains, which in spite of all medical tests indicated no coronary problem, rather than accepting any negative, hostile feelings within herself.

Two cases have been cited to illustrate the effect of the repression of feelings, such as grief, loneliness and anger upon the physical, organic system of the person. Many more could be given. Suffice it to say that physical response to the illness of the person is most readily accessible both to the patient and the physician or counselor. Insight and awareness of the emotional factors that relate to this physical response come with much greater difficulty and are certainly more threatening. But when the patient does gain insight into the stresses and emotional problems that are affecting his physical health, then attempts at resolution will be made, with or without the help of another, professional or otherwise.

ATTEMPTS AT RESOLUTION

Although the patient may gain insight into the relationship of the stressful situations that have contributed to his illness, he will most often attempt to deal with them on the rational rather than the emotional level. Mrs. A. mentioned above could only understand that she had the flu and this contributed to her illness, she could not accept that her grief, loneliness and feelings of uselessness had anything to do with the illness.

Because the prospect of dealing with the emotional problem seems too painful or impossible, one will propose many alternatives to personal change or alteration of life style. For example, he often looks to the physician, the therapist, or counselor to provide "the miracle pill," the quick and painless answer that will clear up everything in the shortest time possible; he may change environment, moving to a new community, making a change in profession or vocation; sometimes he places the burden for change on other persons — parents, spouse and children — being sure that if their ways, habits and mannerisms would conform, then all problems would be solved. All these and any other attempts to manipulate environment or persons more than likely become defenses against changes within one's self which, though painful and difficult, offer perhaps the only possible resolution of the sources of conflict and stress.

As long as the conflict and stress remain unresolved, the illness of such persons becomes chronic. Although not consciously intended to be so, it is entirely possible that the individual is experiencing the secondary gain of attention, care, and sympathy from family and friends. On the other hand it also creates further stress and tensions within the family. So he seeks medical solutions. Not being satisfied with the response of one physician, he goes to another and another, hoping that someone will come up with medication or treatment that will bring about alleviation of the pain and some degree of change. Even though it may not be said in words, the message that he seems to hear is, "It is all in your head; it is your imagination." But the pains are somatic and he is able to define the specific or general areas of the body where he feels them. This can become discouraging, frustrating and lead to some degree of depression. His body hurts and yet the message he gets is that it is all in his mind.

"To say of an illness that it is nervous, functional, due to suggestion is still (wrongly) to many people the same as saying that it is 'imaginary' and that all that is required to rid one's self of it is a little will power" (3).

To seek allevaition of pain only in the body or to attribute it onle to a mental attitude is to fail to consider one's self in terms of wholeness. It is to be hoped that ultimately such an individual might arrive at such insight as to recognize that it is not only my body that has pain, although the pain is real and can be affected organically; or that it is a matter of mental weakness of which I am guilty and worthy only of such labels as hypochondriac, chronic complainer or weakling. But that I am a person and as a person I have pain. I suffer.

"The ideas we are ashamed of, the fears we want to disown, the mistakes and weaknesses we blame ourselves for – all these are the mental and emotional equivalents of bruised bodies and broken limbs needing examination and treatment. If we try to pretend they don't exist or refuse to believe they are really ours, how can we become free of the tensions and disorders they cause" (4). In these words, Fletcher gives a good description of the ailing person or the practitioner – medical, psychological or spiritual – who fails to recognize the total needs of the person and fails to help him to become free of his tensions and disorders. The development of hospital ministries, such as the chapters of this book describe, it evidence that such recognition is becoming more and more a reality with effective interdisciplinary approach to treatment.

THE ROLE OF THE CHAPLAIN IN TREATMENT

What part then does the clergyman, whether serving in a parish or a hospital, contribute to this interdisciplinary approach? There are those (fortunately their numbers are diminishing) who answer "Nothing whatsoever; his job is to save souls."

The record of the Gospels gives clear evidence that the ministry of Jesus was not simply to souls, but to persons, hurting persons, whose hurting was manifest in a variety of ways, physical, emotional and spiritual. It is not a question of *whether* the hospital chaplain or pastor should participate in the total care of the person, but *how* he is to participate and *to what effect.*

The importance of listening in effective pastoral counseling has for some time now been emphasized. In this particular context, however, we emphasize the importance of listening for the pain and the hurting relationships and being alert to clues that the person is suggesting. It seems that it is very important to the person to accept where he is in pain.

It is not necessary to attempt to give a medical diagnosis, for there are those professionally qualified to diagnose and to give treatment. For the chaplain to pretend to do so may be simply an attempt to avoid the task he should be prepared to do. It may not be as important to know where he is hurting in a physical sense, as to help him to share the areas in his life in which he is hurting and to gain insight into their effect on his total well-being.

Such areas may be within his family, between spouse and/or children. It might be that they grow out of stresses on his job, increasing responsibilities, the demands and expectations of superiors, the need to advance by the younger worker which in turn becomes a threat to the position of the older worker. The chaplain will be alert to listen for the loss or threatened loss of meaningful relationships through death, separation, divorce or by children growing up, assuming adult responsibilities and leaving the home. It will be important to know how the patient has or has not handled the loss or how he is facing the prospect of loss. The denial of emotional pain that such situations bring about may be announced by pain in more acceptable ways, such as physical pain.

Mr. G. came to his doctor with complaints of indigestion and dull pain in the abdominal area. After examination, his doctor had him admitted to the hospital with the preliminary diagnosis of gastrointestinal bleeding and chronic depression. After he was admitted, his doctor requested that the chaplain spend as much time with him and see him as frequently as possible. Although he attended the daily patient group meetings on the medical unit, it was soon apparent that it was much more comfortable for him to speak in individual sessions.

His children were grown and no longer lived in the home community. After his wife's death about three years previous, he had moved to a nearby community, away from the small town in which he and his family had lived for many years. He was now living in a room by himself. He continued to work in the same responsible position he had occupied for most of his life which did not require that he live in his home town.

After a few meetings together, it became apparent to the chaplain that Mr. G found the subject of his wife's death and the loneliness he was experiencing to be especially painful. He shared some of the guilt feelings he had both in relationship to her as well as to his children. Now in a matter of a year or two he was facing the prospect of retirement from his job. He seemed to be caught between his unresolved grief over the past and a dismal retirement in the future. He had been suffering alone for sometime. It was not until his suffering became obvious in a physical manner that he sought help from a doctor of internal medicine who was concerned for his whole person and who recognized the problem.

Mr. G. had opportunity to share his feelings of loneliness, guilt, anger, over past situations and his anxiety over the future as he continued to meet with the chaplain; and more and more he was able to share these feelings in the group sessions as well. Ultimately he was discharged from the hospital and returned to his original home community where his friends and his church were. His pastor was informed of the situation by the chaplain and was encouraged to assist Mr. G. to continue making necessary adjustments. He visited a psychiatrist for a few additional sessions and on last report he had no physical complaints and was reestablishing old relationships that he had allowed in the last few years to fall by the wayside.

The emotional stress that resulted in his physical complaints is not unlike that of many other patients who come to the doctor's office or are admitted to the hospital. Admitting to a need for medical help can then become the avenue by which the patient can respond to the opportunity to deal with other stressful areas of his life as well. Perhaps for one of the few times, if not the first time in his life, he can feel open to sharing his feelings and not to deny them or mask them for the protection of others or to uphold an image of himself that he or others have expected of him.

To admit to the intense feelings of loneliness and express them with open tears may be a new experience for one who has long believed that Christians are not to weep at the loss of a loved one. Having learned early in life that not only the expression, but the feeling of anger is sinful, it can be the beginning of a freeing experience to be encouraged by the chaplain to explore these hostile feelings whether to God or others and to begin to talk about them. For the judging of emotions as being good or bad and consequently judging of self as good or bad for having such emotions can be found among so many persons whose physical illnesses are clearly related to their emotional stress. The feelings of anger or grief, guilt or loneliness are considered negative emotions and as such are wrong.

For a long time, it is as if such a person has been saying to himself: "I must not have them; I cannot have them; I will not have them; I do not have them, because they are wrong; they are bad; they are sinful."

He will then strive only for the positive states such as joy, happiness, good cheer, for these are the feelings he has been told by others around him, and he has come to believe, that he should have. At all cost he will be determined to be something that he does not feel within himself to be, and not infrequently the cost will be real physical distress and illness.

As such a person begins to gain insight into the relationship between his emotional stress and physical illness, he can then also begin to discuss with the chaplain some of his misconceptions of moral and spiritual values that he has carried with him into his illness. It is not unusual for patients in religious discussion groups in the hospital or in private conferences to express a desire to be free of the self-rejection, the inner judgment and condemnation that they have so long been experiencing. The rejection of self and the condemnation of self have their counterparts in experiencing rather the acceptance and forgiveness of self. This then opens up the possibility for an experience of the Gospel to become meaningful through the effective ministry of the pastor whether within or outside the hospital. The experience of grace, of forgiveness, becomes the more real on the vertical, the divine-human level and on the horizontal, interpersonal level when it is experienced also intrapersonally, within one's self. This was what Jesus was touching on when He said, "And love your neighbor as yourself."

It is through this experience of grace, of love, of forgiveness that the opportunity for ministry to such persons comes. Now the chaplain will not deal with facts and information about a person but enter into the very communion of his inner feelings, about himself and others which he will now feel free to share. Paul Tournier seems to have had this in mind as he wrote in one of his early writings: "Information speaks of personages. Communion touches the person. Through information I can understand a case, only through communion shall I be able to understand a person. Men expect of us that we should understand them as cases, but they also want to be understood as persons" (5). For such communion that "touches the person" will become for him the experience of forgiveness as an inward, reconciling one, making it possible to move from self-punishment and rejection to a sense of freedom in grace and love in relationship to one's self, to others, and to God.

THE CHAPLAIN AS A MEMBER OF
THE THERAPEUTIC TEAM

As regards the total care of the person who is ill, the chaplain becomes a member of a caring group of people. Not only is his pastoral function important in relationship to the patient, but also with professional persons of other disciplines who are also involved in the care of the patient. The chaplain may have some knowledge of psychology or personality development theory, but he will not presume to function as the patient's psychiatrist or clinical psychologist.

He may have assimilated some basic facts of medical knowledge, but he will be out of his domain if he attempts to answer questions the patient may have concerning his medical, physical problems. Likewise, although he cannot escape at times involvement in the patient's social and family concerns, he will recognize the knowledge and insight of the social worker. It is of utmost importance for the best care possible in the interest of the total needs of the person that the skills and expertise of each team member be recognized, for the achievement of such a goal leaves little or no room for the "prima donna," including the chaplain.

No one can be very long involved in such an interdisciplinary approach to patient care without recognizing that there will be a considerable degree of overlapping. The person and the personality are extremely complex and cannot be divided into neat, clearly-defined divisions, with each professional confined exclusively to the area of his expertise and functioning as though oblivious to the expertise and functioning of other professions, be they medical or paramedical. To be sure, there are those who would like to, and do, attempt to function in this manner. But it is in the sharing of insights and the bringing together of numerous areas of expertise that the more complete needs of the total person can be met.

This, of course, cannot be accomplished if each professional person carries out his responsibilities independently of and without regard for the contributions of another. Some means of communication and method of sharing must be devised which will be best suited to the extent of the resources of a particular institution. The goals of Mr. G., mentioned previously, were not accomplished simply with the request of his doctor that the chaplain visit often with the patient. What took place in the visits? What sharing of feelings and areas of stress were unique in the pastoral relationship that would be beneficial in the total care of Mr. G.? It is entirely possible that he may have shared to some extent with his doctor or the nurse or the social worker, and there is every possibility of some overlapping.

In this particular case, the extent of his "grief-work" and

sharing of his feelings of guilt was greater and, for him, more comfortable in the pastoral relationship. This began initially when the patient was admitted to this particular unit of the hospital to which this chaplain was assigned. But it was more directly focused by the request of the doctor and most satisfactorily fulfilled with the chaplain's participation as a member of the team. Certainly communication takes place with the doctor and the nurse, as well as other members of the team, by individual conversations or by written comments attached to the patient's chart. But it becomes most effective when all members of the caring team can assemble in conference to pool their knowledge and insights. Then treatment goals can be outlined and a common approach developed that can more adequately meet the total care needs of the patient, medically, emotionally, spiritually, and socially.

Westberg supports such a cooperative approach when he says: "No single discipline can care for the whole man, but through active cooperation with other disciplines, something approaching total care is possible . . . such efforts not only enrich the several disciplines, but they also have beneficial results in the improved care of the patient" (6). On the basis of considerable experience on a hospital unit where such total care conferences are an integral part of the program and regularly scheduled, we can give a strong endorsement. The complaint is often voiced by students in clinical training that the hospital staff, including physicians, do not seem to understand the student chaplain's role. It is not unlikely that he is not at all certain of it either, but if he has no opportunity or does not help to create the opportunity that such conferences provide, the valuable contributions that he could be making in total patient care may be missed.

Although his comments are particularly concerned with pastoral ministry in the parish, nevertheless Wayne Oates' *The Christian Pastor* does underscore what we have been saying regarding the hospital team conference as well. "Other professional persons such as doctors . . . social workers, etc. are allies of the pastor. A criterion of effective pastoral work is the willingness and ability of the pastor to function as a fellow minister along with these other persons" (7).

Of course, the conference is not intended as a means for the pastor to establish a clearer role identification for himself (although if he is presuming other roles this may become embarrassingly clear). The sharing of his involvement with the patient on the emotional and spiritual levels, as well as receiving new insights from other disciplines, can contribute to even more effective pastoral care as a part of the total treatment program.

In the total care or ecological program of our hospital, the chaplain is a full-time member of the unit staff. As such he participates with the psychologist, social worker, nursing personnel, dietitian, occupational therapist and others in all staff meetings. Together with the social worker and a member of the nursing staff, he participates in daily patient problem-solving groups and conducts a weekly religious discussion group in which all patients participate.

The chaplain is involved as a professional member of the health care team, for without such involvement other services he may be rendering, important as they may be, will be less effective. Certainly such involvement is not possible in all institutions or in many chaplaincy programs. On the other hand, it is not impossible to believe that with persistence and creative efforts on the part of the chaplain, it can be accomplished to some degree at least.

SUMMARY

Great progress in human development has been made during the present generation and continues to be made, not least in a confrontation by, and a concern for, meeting the many areas of human need. Among these is the treatment of illness which can no longer be confined to the healing of broken, suffering bodies, but greater concern has been shown and progress made in the total treatment of suffering persons. Such developments as we have attempted to point out in this chapter have not been taking place quickly or by waving a magic wand. They continue to take much time and much individual and collective effort on the part of personnel in all disciplines and all the various professionals in the health care field. The increasing number of chaplains in health care facilities and their increasing participation in the total effort bear witness to the recognition of the need to meet the spiritual and emotional problems of the patient as well as his physical and medical needs.

REFERENCES

1. Tournier, Paul: The Meaning of Persons. New York, Harper, 1957. p. 43.
2. Fletcher, Peter: Understanding Your Emotional Problems. New York, Hart. 1958, p. 11.
3. Tournier, Paul: The Person Reborn. New York, Harper, 1966, p. 148.
4. Fletcher: *Ibid*. p. 16.
5. Tournier: *Ibid*. p. 25.
6. Westberg, Granger: Minister and Doctor Meet. New York, Harper, 1961, p. 91.
7. Oates, Wayne: The Christian Pastor. Philadelphia, Westminister, 1964, p. 241.

VIII

PASTORAL CARE OF
THE PSYCHIATRIC PATIENT

WILLARD WAGNER

The real evil in mental disorder is not to be found in the conflict, but is the sense of isolation or estrangement (1).

A NEW perspective is coming in the area of mental health. Perhaps it is a realization of an old truth that the Hebrews had a better grasp of in the Old Testament. This perspective sees man as a whole being. It recognizes man's inter-related biological, psychological, social and spiritual needs. The various healing disciplines which have developed contribute significantly to man's quest for wholeness.

Thus we who have been trained and identify ourselves in the role of pastors do have a unique contribution to make in the field of mental health. It is time we stopped burying this talent and get involved in the healing process and the talent that is ours in the area of dealing with the ultimate, values, goals, self-esteem and self-acceptance. Ernest Bruder lays out as one of his basic assumptions for the establishment of a religious ministry in a mental hospital the following:

> Mental illness, whatever else it is or is not, is basically a religious problem. It is like a fever, an attempt on the part of the personality at cure. It is also a desperate attempt on the part of the individual to keep from selling himself short, or being sold short as a person by his family, friends, society, culture or religion. It is an attempt to keep him from giving up those parts of himself with which he must come to terms and which are essential in his living if he is to become a whole person.
>
> Perhaps this is clearer if we consider that mental health means the wholeness of the individual, a working integration of what he is, what he has been and what he desires to become.

Mental illness, then, is involved with faith — faith in the ultimate, faith in each other, faith in ourselves. Distortion and conflict in any one area affects all areas. Whether it is expressed in religious terms or not, the meaning of life, values, destiny — ultimates — are a matter of faith and therefore are religious concerns. This is the area of the clergyman. Faith proceeds from trust and trust arises from the good relationships that we have with others (2).

An example which illustrates this point follows.

Ann (not her real name) was a patient on the psychiatric unit of Lutheran General Hospital. Following the weekly religious discussion session which the chaplain conducts, Ann asked if she could talk about some religious issues she had been struggling with in her life. She raised the question of heaven and hell. She did not believe that heaven and hell existed in some future tense, as if they were places that she would be sent to following judgment, but rather she believed that heaven and hell existed right here and now in her own life depending on what was happening to her life at that moment. This conflicted, she found, with the views of some of the other patients, and she wondered if it were right for her to hold these views.

This opening question led to a sharing on her part of some of the hells she had experienced in her life. She had recently divorced her husband after several years of tumultous married life in which she had experienced more and more abuse. She spoke of a deprived childhood where she had experienced very little love but a great many demands, along with punishments when she did not fulfill the demands.

After a number of sessions where we dealt with the issue of self worth and acceptability, she came to share what she considered to be her final secret and the one that had led her to attempt to take her life before coming to the hospital. Her secret was that she had been a prostitute before marriage. She had used this as a means of escape from the loveless home she had experienced; this was the hell she had gone through in her brief life of some 20 years, and her concern as she shared this with me was would the chaplain accept her even knowing this about her past. The intense feelings that she had about herself (as she was able to share this) were guilt, worthlessness and a need to be punished.

At the same time that Ann was sharing her secret with the

she also shared it with her psychiatrist and the social worker, in a way testing each of them to get their reaction to her. As this came to our attention, we as a staff were able to better understand what it was that Ann was struggling with in her life and also we were able to be more consistent in our approach with her.

Each of the therapeutic team played an important role in Ann's treatment and recovery. The psychiatrist, through the use of medication and psychotherapy, assisted Ann to cope and resolve some of the conflicts that caused her to become depressed.

The social worker was supportive of Ann and assisted her in locating a new job. Before her hospitalization she was involved in work that was very demanding of her both physically and emotionally. It was felt both by Ann and by the team that a new job which was not so emotionally draining might assist her in coping with her depression.

The chaplain continued to work with Ann around the key religious issues that she raised, namely, "If I am unacceptable to myself, how can another person accept me and beyond that, how can God accept me as I am?"

The word that comes to mind in describing the ministry is "incarnational." It was a "being with" that enabled acceptance to be given not only with the spoken word but with the "personal word" that gives the other the strength to take a new look at herself and to see herself in a new light, without a need to continue to punish herself and to feel guilty. As Ann experienced this acceptance, she was able to begin to know in a real way that God did care for her in all of her humanity. This led Ann to begin to experience herself not as an unforgivable person but rather as a unique individual who has value and a sense of worth both in the sight of God and in her own eyes. In experiencing that, life took on new meaning for Ann and she was able to move out in relationship to others.

PREDOMINANT RELIGIOUS ISSUES

One of the constant themes that is brought up in discussion of religious topics held weekly on each unit (particularly from those who have been recently admitted) is, "God certainly must be punishing me. Why would He have me end up in this place?"

There is a strong feeling that they are the guilty ones, they have failed the people on the outside and they have failed themselves and thus they deserve — they feel — to be punished by God. It is only as they are accepted and to begin to deal responsibly with the many emotional aspects of their lives that they begin to regain their self-love and to sense God as loving and caring rather than as punishing and demanding.

A second religious issue that is voiced by the emotionally troubled is the feeling that they are cut off from or are very distant in their relationship to God. This issue has been voiced repeatedly by those who have experienced a close relationship to God in the past. Suddenly they find in the midst of their emotional troubles, when they sense very desperately a need to reach out to God for support, He is not there the way He was before for them. Where before He was very close and involved in their lives in a meaningful way, He now is distant, removed and unmoving. Or so it seems to the person undergoing the pain of an emotional breakdown.

There are numerous examples of persons who have voiced their concern both in the religious discussions on the unit, in individual sessions and in the group therapy sessions. One which stands out was a pastor's wife who characterized her life prior to coming to the hospital as a life of giving to others. For years she had taken an active part in the church program: teaching, leading a Bible study, calling on shut-ins, and being involved in the activities of the parish. What embarrassed her most of all was that for many years she had taught others that they should trust in the Lord and now she found that she had a hard time trusting in Him because she felt that she was totally cut off from God.

Along with the loneliness of being cut off from God she also experienced loneliness of being out of touch with other people and with herself. There even came a point in her life where she gave up going to church, one of the things she had enjoyed most. The only way that she could describe her emotional state was to say that she was afraid — afraid of others and afraid of what might happen if she were to go. Her dilemma was that on the one hand she felt a strong pull to be close both to God and to her fellow humans and on the other hand she was afraid of getting close to others, afraid that she would be overpowered and that she would lose herself among others.

From this perspective, the religious issue that presents itself in the midst of this loneliness and the quest for a closer relationship with God and fellow human beings in the absence of that relationship is the loss of faith.

The question that is so frequently raised by disturbed patients is, Why don't I feel close to God anymore? Why is God so distant, so unreachable, so uninvolved in my life? One aspect that comes to the fore is the sense of loss that they are experiencing in their lives at this moment. They have lost their relationship to God, their ability to trust and love Him, to have faith in Him, and they have lost their ability to trust, to have faith in and to love themselves.

Reuel Howe, in his book *The Miracle of Dialogue,* cast some light on this issue when he wrote, "the tragedy that attends interrupted dialogue as a natural consequence of broken relationship and death of the person is the loss of God. God is dead. He is not really, of course; but to the monological person who, like the Pharisee, stands 'praying thus with himself; God seems to be dead. Life is no longer rich in possibility; now it is only a formulation wrapped up in habit and stored in the closet of religion' (3).

What can restore or renew the faith that was lost? What can bring forth life in a person who feels God is dead? From personal experience, what has proven to be effective is the ministry of listening, listening that is *not* passively sitting with another as he rambles on about his life and its tribulation, but instead a listening that involves one's whole self with the self of another as he searches to find release from his loneliness.

It is listening that actively involves both of them in the patient's struggle to once more have faith in himself as a person and to have faith in God who is the Lord and Giver of Life. When that kind of listening takes place, a listening that accepts, prizes and affirms the person, then the "miracle of dialogue" that Howe talks about takes place, and the miracle is that a person is reborn, he comes to life again and begins to sense the possibilities that are his because of his uniqueness and worth as a human being.

When that takes place in the lives of those who feel cut off from God, then the words of Isaiah take on flesh and blood where he writes, "The Spirit of the Lord God is upon me, because the Lord has anointed me to bring good tidings to the afflicted; he has sent me to bind up the broken hearted, to proclaim liberty to the

captives, and the opening of the prison to those who are bound."
(Isaiah 61:1)

As the chaplain spoke with the pastor's wife, a theme that
recurred in the conversations was that of worthlessness. From her
description of her life and work in the parish, it seemed as if she
had given and given to others until the well had run dry and there
was nothing left to give, not only to others but to herself. She felt
that she was not worth bothering with and thus it surprised and
amazed her when people from the parish continued to indicate
their care and concern for her. It appeared that her limited faith in
herself before hospitalization did not allow her the freedom to
deal responsibly with some of the demands that were placed on
her nor with the anger that resulted. The end result for her was to
be overwhelmed by it all. She coped in the only way that was
acceptable to her and that was to withdraw – withdrawing from
being in touch with herself and her feelings, withdrawing from
meaningful relationship with others and withdrawing from God.

Somewhere in the early years of her life she had learned a
hearsay that is quite prevalent in the church. That hearsay is
something like this: "A Christian shouldn't feel proud nor should
a Christian express negative feelings because we are to be humble
and loving at all times."

Yet she did not always feel loving toward her husband, who
found himself caught up in the demands of the parish and had
very little left in terms of time and emotional energy to give to his
wife. Nor did she feel very loving toward herself when she
experienced others as more important than herself. That in fact
made her very angry and upset but she could not honestly share
those feelings. So she swallowed them until they devoured her
own faith in herself and in her God, with the result that she was
left empty.

In the care and treatment of her, listening was no easy task for
the various members of the team. The message she repeatedly gave
to the psychiatrist, chaplain, nurses and social worker could be
best characterized in the words, "Woe is me, I don't know why
things are so terrible for me."

The chaplain, relating to her, entered into dialogue with her, a
dialogue that not only listened to her "Woe is me," but also

listened for that which was uniquely hers as a person and encouraged her to begin to express it particularly in relationship to her husband. At times the listening took the form of confrontational listening, indicating to her that she had been heard, and yet also confronting her with other possibilities and ways of handling her anger than always swallowing it, until it in turn devoured her and made her feel worthless.

Her recovery was slow and painful. In the end the chaplain learned from ministering to her what it meant to be patient, while she learned what it meant to be more fully human and that God accepted her in that humanness and that it was good both in His sight and in hers.

The third religious issue that the chaplain can and should deal with in relationship to the deeply troubled is that of "meaning in life." For the most part in my work as a chaplain, I have held that if a person has no self-identity, no sense of self-worth, if he is not able to perceive his uniqueness as a person among others, then he cannot find a sense of direction of meaning for his life.

"If I am meaningless, then life is meaningless as well." Maybe the reverse is also true. If I have no direction, no goal, no purpose toward which to strive then I also feel that way about myself as a person. Or to put it into more positive terms, when I have a goal for my life, when I have formulated an overall meaning for my life, then I have a sense of identity and value which makes life worthwhile.

This was brought to my attention as I counseled with a couple having marital problems. The relationship had broken down and there was little that either could perceive as positive in the marriage. Their main reason for continuing in the relationship at this point after 18 years of marriage was "for the sake of the children."

It was in response to the question, When was there a time that both of you felt close or that you had a meaningful relationship, that the wife recalled (and the husband agreed) that it was when she had been carrying their last child. The wife during this pregnancy was seriously ill. Primarily physically at first, but later in the pregnancy she became depressed and it was during this time that the husband became much more involved both because he was concerned for his wife and because of the demands of the household.

The goal that caught up both of them was "to get through this illness." As they sought to attain that goal, their relationship became from the wife's vantage point, the closest that it had ever been in their married life. There was more concern shown, more sharing taking place and more positive regard for each other.

The goal transformed their married life into a relationship that was meaningful and it lasted as long as they had a goal in sight. When the goal had been achieved, they returned to the old patterns of relating to each other. The tragedy of this was not that they returned to their old patterns but that their goal was not large enough to assist them to have an ongoing and meaningful relationship.

It is to this emotional/religious issue of meaning in life that the Christian faith and pastoral care can speak in such a way so as to assist the deeply troubled to find a goal that will give meaning and purpose to their lives.

Robert Leslie, in his book *Jesus and Logotherapy*, puts it very succinctly when he says, "A person realizes his fullest potentiality when he commits himself to a task great enough to call upon all of his talents and abilities" (4).

Pastoral care, when dealing with this issue, is to assist the person to find a goal to which he can commit himself and which in turn will make life for him meaningful and worthwhile. The words of the apostle Paul are applicable to not only the deeply troubled but to all of us when he says, "work out your salvation with fear and trembling." It is an awesome task to struggle with the tensions and conflicts that arise in our life and we need to continually work toward the goal to become more complete, whole persons in a fragmented world.

MINISTERING TO STAFF

One very practical aspect of the work of a chaplain on a psychiatric floor is his ministry to others who are a part of the healing team. This means that the wholeness that is desired for the patient is not so very much different from the wholeness that we work for among the team of psychiatrists, social workers, nursing staff, occupational and recreational therapists and chaplains.

Unless there is a trust of one another, an openness in the dialogue and a comprehensive goal which gives a sense of direction, we, like the very ones we work with, end up frustrated, lonely and not sure where we are in our work and in our relationship to each other. One aspect of the work then on the unit is to minister not only to the patients and their needs but to minister — give pastoral care — to staff members so that they can be in fact a healing community caring for the whole person.

This ministry to the staff has taken the form at times of support for that member of the staff who is experiencing grief over the loss of a loved one. The support given to the nurse who lost her son was a proclamation of the Gospel by being with her, by sharing in her grief and by assisting her to express some of the anger that she felt toward God and toward others.

There is also support given to those who are finding a particular patient hard to cope with at times, due either to the person's behavior or to something that gets triggered within the staff person. In some instances, it is the staff who assists the chaplain, by ministering to his need so that he can have a clearer perspective in his relating to an individual patient who is frustrating him and he is not sure as to why or what is going on in the relationship.

At other times the chaplain's ministry to staff is assisting to resolve conflict that comes out of working closely together with others. In many ways the chaplain's ministry to staff has much the quality of the parish pastor. The chaplain's parish are the members of the healing team and the patients.

It is to these that the chaplain comes to listen to them, to assist them to find their own uniqueness as persons and to help them find a goal or purpose in life that is big enough to give to them a sense of meaning and value.

REFERENCES

1. Boisen, Anton: The Exploration of the Inner World. New York, Harper, 1962, p. 268.
2. Bruder, Ernest: Ministering to Deeply Troubled People. Philadelphia, Fortress Press, 1964, p. 28.
3. Howe, Reuel: The Miracle of Dialogue. New York, Seabury Press, 1963, p. 87.
4. Leslie, Robert: Jesus and Logotherapy. Nashville, Abingdon, Press, 1965, p. 66.

IX

CHAPLAINCY TO ALCOHOLICS

JOHN E. KELLER

ALCOHOLICS are not admitted in many hospitals. When they are admitted with another diagnosis, the alcoholism usually is not identified. Even when identified, many doctors neither realistically deal with it nor make an adequate referral.

First you must believe that alcoholism is a specific, identifiable, progressive, fatal illness that requires specific treatment. Then it is quite apparent that ignoring it, bypassing it, treating it purely symptomatically or handling it with some talk about drinking too much is not good for the patient.

Chances are good that what has just been said about the doctors also is valid for many pastors, chaplains and chaplain supervisors as well as other professional personnel. Education and training in alcoholism treatment is still not a part of many clinical pastoral training experiences.

The hospital chaplain can be a key person in beginning to deal realistically with the alcoholic patient and enhance the possibility of the alcoholic getting some kind of treatment consideration. He may also be instrumental in getting hospital administration and other staff interested to the point where alcoholics will be admitted and realistic treatment will be provided for these sick people.

Because alcoholism is not just a symptomatic illness, special education and training in alcoholism are essential. There is much not yet known about alcoholism and alcoholism treatment, but there is a large body of information and experience that demonstrates alcoholism is treatable and the prognosis for recovery better than many realize. As a chaplain exposes himself to learning about alcoholism and to clinical experience with alcoholics and their families, he will learn how to be comfortable with alcoholics and deal directly with the alcoholism.

87

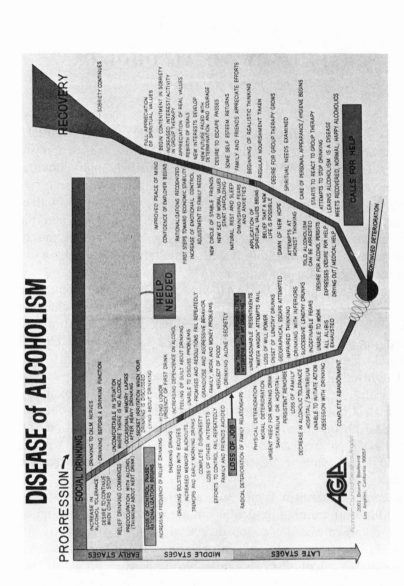

Figure 1. Progressive symptom chart on alcoholism.

One basic source of information is this progressive symptom chart on alcoholism. To know the groupings of progressive symptoms is essential to having meaningful conversation regarding the drinking. Out of this comes a natural kind of "listening ear" that picks up descriptive information about the extent of progression in the drinking problem and especially the feelings and defense mechanisms around the drinking that reveal the alcoholism.

Extensive information about the nature of alcoholism will not be given here. That is readily available to any interested chaplain. Information about training possibilities can be received from the national or regional offices of the Association for Clinical Pastoral Education or Alcohol and Drug Problems Association of North America.

Most of the alcoholism a chaplain would be confronted with would be marked by the phenomenon of "loss of control." A brief description of this reality and its significance in terms of caring for the alcoholic is important.

Many people drink and in a variety of ways because they want to drink, and their drinking never becomes a problem. That is *drinking.* Some people get drunk sometimes or frequently because they want to get drunk. That's *drunkenness.*

Some people drink excessively in response to problems. That's *problem drinking.* Some people drink excessively because they can no longer drink within their own intention. That is a *drinking problem* – loss of control – the most prominent kind of alcoholism. Obviously all of this is a simplification, but it is also an easily understood and workable description.

Loss of control is identifiable as both the inability to control the drinking and the inability to quit drinking. The best such alcoholics can do on their own is delay the next out-of-control drinking experience. Loss of control, on the basis of present clinical information and experience, is generally to be considered as a permanent, irreversible, progressive reality. A person either has it or does not have it. Just as a woman cannot be a little bit pregnant, so a person cannot be a little bit alcoholic with loss of control. He is or he is not. The only difference is where he might be in the progression. And when loss of control is present, the excessive drinking is not just a symptomatic phenomenon but also a specific illness needing direct treatment.

When loss of control is a reality, then what the psychiatrist, psychologist, social worker or chaplain may think the underlying problems are does have importance but is not primary. The immediate problem is the drinking problem.

The downward progression is evitable in every area of this person's life. Few illnesses so inevitably and progressively affect the total relationships and life of a human being as alcoholism. As with diabetes, cancer, high blood pressure, heart disease, something direct needs to be done about the specific illness of alcoholism.

When a person has loss of control, he is generally incapable of seeing and especially doing something about any other basic problems he has. He will want to believe he does not have a drinking problem, and if he admits it is a problem, he will want to deal with it symptomatically. The person who has alcoholism is a person who generally is not available for other help he might need until he becomes available for help with the alcoholism. Clinically there appear to be very few exceptions to this. Any insight he may gain into himself prior to acceptance of the alcoholism is generally not internalized and does not result in behavior change.

Initial involvement, including pastoral function, is to help the person become aware of the alcoholism, the need for treatment and hopefully in the process hasten the day when he or she will take the first step towards treatment.

Besides knowing how to do this, one primary requirement is a nonmoralistic attitude. This from a chaplain may have more significance than from any other professional helper. Alcoholics, with apparently few exceptions, are essentially moralists. This is their strong internal response to the out-of-control drinking. The church historically had the same response — get him to realize how sinful his drinking is and then you can help him. Even if the church historically would have had a nonmoralistic response, the alcoholic because of his own moralizing about his condition would have expected such an attitude.

In many cases the chaplain can more readily dispel the moralistic response than can other helpers, not by what he says but through his attitude of accepting alcoholism as an illness. It is tragic that Christianity for so many is synonymous with a moralistic attitude and way of life. When a chaplain through his understanding and attitudes can be instrumental in dispelling this perception of alcoholism and the alcoholic, he has rendered a most necessary and meaningful pastoral service for alcoholics. When the chaplain also has internal freedom to let the alcoholic continue to drink if he desires and to let the alcoholic be responsible for his drinking problem, then relationship with the alcoholic can be readily established.

Initially it is important to keep the focus on the drinking because that is the immediate problem. Generally it can be assumed that either Scripture and prayer or primary conversation about other problems become ways for both the chaplain and the alcoholic to avoid the immediate reality of the alcoholism.

If the chaplain is in a hospital that admits alcoholics, then he would quite obviously be talking with the patient about his drinking problem. If the patient has a drinking problem but is admitted under a different diagnosis, then the chaplain needs to initiate conversations about the patients drinking. (If the chaplain does any marital counseling, the question as to whether or not drinking is any kind of a problem is best raised early in the counseling process. A drinking problem frequently may be present but not mentioned by the couple.)

When a person has or may have a drinking problem, as much descriptive information as possible about the drinking is to be obtained from the spouse or significant other. When a person has alcoholism, the chaplain can function with two assumptions that are almost always valid: (a) Part if not all of the drinking the person does is bothering him; (b) The person assumes that identification of a drinking problem has to do with the ability "to take it or leave it" rather than the phenomenon of inability to control the drinking.

When having conversations about the drinking, the patient will usually express both of these in some way. If not, the chaplain needs to find a way to bring these to the surface.

Alcoholics classically seek to get and to keep the conversation off the drinking onto something or someone else. If the conversation focuses on the drinking, they are usually involved in a process of denial and minimization.

Here is a very simple and generally effective way to get and keep the focus on the drinking.

Chaplain: "I notice, Bill, that there is some indication of a possible drinking problem." (The chaplain may know he came in intoxicated or may have seen evidence of withdrawal symptoms or read physician's notes on liver condition.) "In talking with your wife, she said that you know she thinks you have a drinking problem. How do you feel about it?"

The spouse has described a serious daily pattern of excessive drinking with missing work during last two years and two other hospitalizations. If the spouse says he has a drinking problem but asks the chaplain not to let her husband know she told the chaplain, it is necessary to help the spouse realize that it is important to get this out in the open.

Patient: "She's always fussing about something. If it isn't my drinking, its something else. I had a few before I came in today, but I've been having these pains in my leg lately and a few drinks seem to help."

Chaplain: "According to your records it was more than just a few, Bill. You were really pretty well saturated with alcohol."

Patient: "Yeah, well sometimes I drink too much, but it's no real problem." (He has now said he drinks too much sometimes.) "I can take it or leave it and once they find out what's causing this leg pain, I'll be O.K."

Chaplain: "As long as you feel you can take it or leave it, you figure your drinking is no problem. Is that it?"

Patient: "Well, that's true isn't it? I know guys who really are hooked on the stuff. They gotta drink in the morning to get settled down, and they drink all day. They couldn't quit if they wanted to."

Chaplain: "What kind of drinking do you do, Bill?"

Patient: "What do you mean?"

Chaplain: "Well, sometimes you obviously drink too much. How about other times when you drink? What kind of drinking do you do?"

Patient: "Oh, I usually have a few when I get home from work. Or if I'm watching a ball game I may have a six-pack. There have been some days when I haven't had anything at all to drink."

Chaplain: "What happens then on these occasions like this last one?"

Patient: "Like I told you, this pain in my leg. Sometimes it gets so bad I drink to kill the pain."

Chaplain: "You mean you intended to drink yourself into the kind of shape you were in when they brought you to the hospital?"

Patient: "No, not that. That was just too much."

Chaplain: "Well how do you explain to yourself drinking that much?"

Patient: "I don't know. It just happens once in awhile."

Chaplain: "How do you feel when that happens, Bill?"

Patient: "You mean when I drink too much?"

Chaplain: "Yes."

Patient: "Not very good."

Chaplain: "You don't like yourself when you do that."

Patient: "That's right. But I know I can take it or leave it."

Chaplain: "Well, Bill, I don't know if you know it or not, but the key question isn't whether you can take it or leave it. The key question is whether you have lost control – whether you drink the way you do sometimes because you can't control the amount you drink."

Patient: "There are a lot of times I drink when that doesn't happen."

Chaplain: "No, but it happens sometimes, that, as you said earlier, you drink a lot more than you intended to."

(This conversation would continue with further information on the loss of control phenomenon, not knowing what causes it, that it happens to about 1 out of 12 who drink in our society, and when it happens, this is a permanant, irreversible, progressive reality that is called alcoholism.)

Chaplain: "Do you think, Bill, you could drink with control within certain limits you would set, for a period of say three months?"

Patient: "I am sure I could."

Chaplain: "That would be the way to find out if you have loss of control or not. Do you think you would be interested in finding out?"

Patient: "Yeah, I think so. What do you think would be a good limit?"

Chaplain: "Well, I don't know. What do you think would be appropriate for you? On any day you drink, how many drinks?"

Patient: "Oh, I don't know, maybe four or five."

Chaplain: "That sounds O.K. If you haven't lost control, Bill, you will be able to do that. But if you have lost control over your drinking, you won't be able to do it for three months. You will go off the deep end. Now it is important not to make a big deal out of this like you are going to prove to yourself or show your wife. It is much better to have the attitude of let's find out."

Patient: "Sounds good to me."

Chaplain: "Before going any further with this, Bill, I want to share with you that it looks very much to me that your drinking is well into alcoholism, probably the early part of the late stage of alcoholism. What I would like to do is bring you some more information, have you look at it and then discuss it with you. Then, by the time you are discharged, if you still think you don't have loss of control, you can try this three-months deal. How do you react to this idea."

Patient: "O.K. I don't mind, but I really think I'll be able to handle it."

It may be that the patient will be ready for a direct referral for treatment from the hospital, and a visit from a member of Alcoholics Anonymous (A.A.). If not the chaplain can share with the patient information on in-patient, out-patient services for alcoholism, A.A., and also Al-anon for spouse.

This is information he needs to have in a preliminary way along with his decision to try the three-month idea of controlled drinking in case he does not make it. The chaplain can suggest that if he does not make the three months, the patient give him a call for further conversations. Sometimes it is necessary to go a second time with an alcoholic on the three-month test in order for him to accept more conclusively the reality of alcoholism. However, if a second attempt at controlled drinking is desired by the alcoholic, there is no reason why the chaplain cannot affirm his own diagnosis of alcoholism after failure in the first effort.

Once a person who has "loss of control" hears that phrase with a description, he does not forget it, even if he is refusing to accept the reality of alcoholism. Such information is part of a seed-planting process that can significantly spoil his drinking and hopefully hasten the day he seeks help.

When the wife or husband is convinced the spouse has alcoholism, it is important that he/she get actively involved in Al-anon. If this involvement does not result in significant learning together with necessary attitude and behavior change, then there is good possibility that the spouse has some deep-seated problems for which professional help is needed but may not be too effective.

Once an alcoholic is ready to accept his alcoholism and get involved in treatment, then the chaplain's primary function is referral to in-patient, out-patient services and/or Alcoholics Anonymous. The process of being involved with the alcoholic and focusing on the drinking problem does not need to be a time consuming process as is so often indicated if the chaplain will make use of other resources in the community.

A significant part of any chaplain's education and training in alcoholism is reading the A.A. and Al-anon books and extensive exposure to their meetings to get the feel of the process and experience, as well as to become acquainted with recovering alcoholics and their spouses. Since A.A. and Al-anon involve a new way of life which is essentially spiritual in content, this will have special interest and significance for the chaplain.

If a chaplain will provide himself adequate education and training together with ongoing direct experience in counseling alcoholic patients and their families, he can find this to be an enriching experience for himself, his learning and his ministry.

X

MINISTRY TO STAFF

ARTHUR BICKEL and BRUCE HARTUNG

THE patient had been in the hospital six weeks. In surgery a tumor had been removed from her bowel, and a colostomy had been performed. The incision healed slowly because of an infection. It healed so slowly that the surgeons suspected a recurrence of the cancer. The recurrence of cancer was confirmed by tests. The patient had been told and had been depressed for several days.

When the chaplain came on the floor one morning, the patient's nurse happened to be at the desk. He asked her about the patient. She shared some observations and then continued.

"I've got a problem with her. I've allowed myself to get too involved. This morning when she talked about herself, I got so choked up, I had to excuse myself and go out of the room to pull myself together. I'm so close to her, I can't help her and that's not good."

The conversation continued, during which both the nurse and the chaplain shared some of the anger and depression over this patient's plight. The problem was discussed of trying to be open enough to care, yet not so identified with the patient that it becomes almost impossible to help.

This conversation occurred in the hospital. It is shared as an example of ministry to a hospital nurse. It demonstrates aspects of three themes which will be examined in this chapter:

1. Common concerns of the staff as demonstrated in group meetings with nurses.
2. Oportunities for ministry.
3. Basic assumptions underlying staff ministry.

This is a description of a consultation session with the nursing personnel of a medical unit, led by one of the authors. The description is a relatively loose one, since an agenda is obviously not identical from week to week in any group. The purpose of presenting the description is to give an idea of how this one particular group operated, with the suggestion that such a methodology be changed to local conditions but implemented where possible.

Basically, a consultation model was followed. One and a half hours were set aside where the chaplain would meet with those members of the nursing staff (registered nurses, licensed practical nurses, aides and orderlies) who were available and who wanted to meet. The responsibility for what was brought to the session was with the nursing personnel. The chaplain functioned only as a resource.

The idea was that the nursing personnel would bring to the session the concerns that they had concerning their interactions with certain patients on the floor. Those reactions could then be discussed in light of the personality of the patient and the personality characteristics of the nursing personnel. In some instances, suggestions were made concerning treatment and management techniques for the nurses in relationship to the patients.

The contract was clearly not an interpersonal relations contract. Clinical material, external to the interaction of the group, was most often the issue of the day. However in such a presentation, interpersonal styles of the nursing personnel could become an issue and were never ignored. The consultation model was used, however, so that the primary focus would remain the care of the patient. The opportunity might then be taken to use the interaction between nurse and patient as a chance to discuss reactions and personal feelings in relationship to the patient.

The chaplain functioned basically in two ways. He was the facilitator who both raised issues about the patient and reflected "feeling" issues as they arose in the session. When the issues about the patient were raised, some small theoretical input on occasion was provided. When discussing the terminal patient, the dynamics of grief were often talked about. With the presentation of an amputee, the process of grief as it affected loss of a limb was discussed. This input was in no way an extended lecture. On occasion, it did provide the base for a discussion of nursing care and the jumping-off point for a dynamic understanding of the patient.

On the other hand, nurses' feelings, either in relationship to a patient or in relationship to another staff person, at times became the dominant concern. For instance, in one session the patient was a young man dying of terminal cancer. Not only did this allow for a discussion of the care of a terminally ill patient but also the feelings of the nursing personnel concerning this young man were explored. A number of feelings were expressed including fear of losing control while in the room, identifying with the patient, and anger at the stroke of fate (or the providence of God) that would allow such a thing to happen. This session gave the nursing personnel an opportunity to ventilate their emotions and to look at how they could constructively use their feelings to help the patient deal with his concerns and be cared for during the last days of his life.

In another instance, an elderly woman who was making a number of the nursing personnel angry at her was discussed. She was very demanding, "too dependent" from the nurses' point of view. During the session both the nurses' desire to have people depend on them and their anger at being depended upon too much so that it became a burden were discussed and explored.

The chaplain was not afraid to supply input materials to the nursing staff. Feelings of the staff members were not ignored, but were encouraged to be expressed openly. With this methodology the chaplain helped prepare the staff personnel for a relevant ministry to people in need.

OPPORTUNITIES FOR STAFF MINISTRY

The most apparent opportunities for staff ministry occur in scheduled, planned meetings with individual staff members or groups. Probably more opportunities occur informally when the chaplain is sensitive to the needs of staff members if they find him to be an understanding, warm pastor with integrity.

When an individual staff member wants to talk, the chaplain needs to assess whether it is advisable to talk alone, and whether the matter being discussed will require more time, perhaps several scheduled hours.

A brief encounter requiring no further planned ministry is

illustrated by the chaplain who saw one of the cleaning personnel in the hall.

Chaplain: "Hello, Mary."
Staff: "Hi, Chaplain."
Chaplain: "You look happy today,"
Staff: "I am. I didn't know it was showing so much. I've told you about our son. We got a letter from him yesterday. He got accepted into graduate school. He's wanted this very much because he feels he has to have a graduate degree to get a good job."
Chaplain: "That's good news."
Staff: "You bet. We're happy that he can continue studying. You know I don't really have to work except I want to help him a bit with money for school. He appreciates that. So we've all kind of been working together for this."
Chaplain: "It's an accomplishment for all of you."
Staff: "Yes, Besides that, we've decided to take a trip to visit him for graduation, and then my husband and I are going on to California for a couple of weeks. Maybe that's making me so happy."

The conversation closed in a few moments with comment about having much to thank God for and each went on to work. Much of the chaplain's ministry occurs in such brief, informal encounters with individuals.

At other times, it is apparent that the staff person needs more opportunity to talk.

The chaplain stopped at the nursing station to inquire about a patient. As he left, a nurse stopped him quietly.

Nurse: "Pastor, can I talk to you sometime?
Chaplain: "Sure. Want to talk here or would you rather come to my office?"
Nurse: "In your office. It's kind of private and I'd rather no one up here knew about it."
Chaplain: "O.K. What would be a good time?"
Nurse: "Well it's not real urgent. Are you free when I get off at 3:30? Sometime this week or next?"

An appointment was made and her need for confidence was respected. She was having problems in her marriage and several hours of marriage counseling ensued. The chaplain gave her the opportunity to state her need for more private time. Sometimes it is possible only after the chaplain has talked privately with a staff member to assess the need for further time.

Ministry to groups can occur informally. At a nursing station two nurses, an intern, a service secretary and a chaplain happened to meet. The nurse was discussing a decision by a surgeon made moments earlier, not to perform surgery on a critical elderly patient who was bleeding rectally.

The nurse and the intern felt the patient had a slim chance to survive surgery. The chaplain raised the question of whether the patient had a right to die without further pain. Before the conversation was finished, the secretary, several other nurses and another intern had participated in the converstaion. Issues of the right to live or die, where responsibility lies, and the meaning of death, were talked about before the group had to break up. The result of the conversation was that the two interns who knew the surgeon urged him to reconsider surgery, and he eventually decided to do it. The patient recovered and was discharged.

The nursing station is a frequent site for informal group meetings in which the chaplain can participate, and sometimes offer a vital ministry. Similar opportunities for informal group ministry may occur at lunch when a group of personnel talk about some aspect of their work or the institution.

A variety of structured group meetings occur which lend themselves to staff ministry. The weekly staff group meetings described earlier in the chapter above have been particularly effective. Though the issues discussed in these meetings center primarily about patient care concerns, some matters related to staff relationships as well as individual personal concern are shared and talked about in the meetings.

Nursing report meetings at the changing of shifts are particularly rich in staff ministry opportunities. A typical participation for the chaplain in a report meeting might proceed as follows, after the physical condition of the patient and all orders have been reported.

Nurse: "Mr. Wills has been quite depressed ever since he came in. I don't know why. He's quite irritable and hard to take care of for that reason."

Chaplain: "I spent some time with him today and he shared some of the troubles he's had lately. Has he talked with any of you about them?"

Nurses: "Very little."
Chaplain: "He's worried about being laid off at work. They've laid off a lot of the employees lately. He knows he has quite a bit of seniority, but he's still worried. Also his wife is home recuperating from some surgery. He had to get friends and relatives to help take care of her when he came to the hospital, and he wants very much to be at home. I don't think this is confidential, but it might be wise to treat it as such until he brings it up with you."
Nurse: "That's good to know. At least, we can be a little more understanding of him."

If particularly difficult problems arise in report meetings, it might be appropriate for the chaplain to suggest a staff meeting of crucial personnel to discuss a certain patient. (These sessions are called ecology meetings at Lutheran General Hospital and are initiated by any personnel who feel the need for them.) At the meeting one person is asked to present the crucial information on the patient which precipitates the ensuing discussion.

Any formal planned meetings in which the chaplain participates may also offer opportunities for his ministry.

Underlying Assumptions of Staff Ministry

Probably the most profound and maybe also the most debatable basic assumption of ministry to staff is that ministry in a broad sense belongs to all the people of God. It is the responsibility and privilege of the whole "body of Christ." The New Testament and particularly St. Paul emphasize the importance of the corporate ministry. Within the Protestant arm of the Christian Church, this concept has been described in the doctrine of the royal priesthood. Roman Catholics, though wary of that kind of terminology, have been emphasizing particularly since Vatican II the importance of individual commitment to serve.

The hospital ideally is staffed by people who care about others and who are committed to serve others. In a very real sense, hospital personnel are ministers and the chaplain's work is a "ministry to ministers." It may be so that some of the service-care motivation among hospital staff has faded in recent years, but service still remains a vital motivating force within many who work in hospitals. The fact that there may be some loss of service motivation is a challenge to the chaplaincy department of institutions to encourage and support the desire to serve. It seems that it would appropriately be of vital concern to church-related or religiously-oriented institutions to maintain a high level of service motivation. The chaplains can be key persons in helping maintain this high level.

A second vital assumption which makes the ministry to staff essential is that the personnel who spend the most time with the patient or in the patient's room also have the most frequent and ideal opportunities to serve. It is an exception when the chaplain spends an hour with a patient, but it is routine for the nursing staff to spend that much time with patients in the morning when giving baths and changing the bedding.

In institutions where registered nurses are in short supply, the aides may have the most extended contact with patients. The depth of relationships which sometimes develops between various staff members and patients is often apparent when patients are discharged and they speak of their sincere appreciation to the personnel. It behooves the hospital to encourage and develop the skills of personnel in relational ministry to patients, and the chaplain can make an important contribution to that end. Perhaps a crucial step would be to communicate to the staff that he believes they can do some things as well or better in ministering to the spiritual needs of patients.

A third assumption supporting the importance of ministry to staff is that much effective ministry can and does occur in brief encounters. We are influenced today by the explosion of knowledge and consequent specialization, and these developments have contributed to an assumption that not much is accomplished unless an effort is intense and profound. However, this represents something of a distortion.

For instance, the steady influence of parents on children, mostly in a series of many brief encounters, influences in depth the emotional development of a child. There are few, if any, weekly one-hour or more intense conferences scheduled in which the parent serves as a counselor to his child. This does not belittle the value of counseling. The point is that in the parent-child relationship where influence is profound, that influence occurs primarily in many brief encounters. The chaplain does well to recognize the possibilities of a significant ministry to staff in the many brief encounters he has daily with staff members.

Another assumption underlying ministry to staff is that the chaplain has skills in pastoral care which can be used by other personnel in ministering to patients. Basic concepts will be helpful to personnel, such as recognizing the establishment of rapport, the art of disciplined listening and the process of reflection, the skills and problems of accurate empathy, the crucial nature of warm, nonmanipulative interest in patients, common pitfalls such as attempting to give premature or unwanted advice, agreeing or disagreeing when acceptance is needed, overidentification, focusing on problems and answers on only a verbal behavior.

Personnel who feel free to discuss their service to patients with the chaplain are often receptive to the chaplain's support and to any learning or growth which might occur in discussions with him. It should not be construed that hospital staff become masters of another profession. It is true, however, that some persons have innate sensitivity to others and with a little informed help can become even more skillful at responding to not only physical but also emotional and spiritual needs of patients.

A final reality which creates the need for staff ministry is the fact that all personnel in a hospital are continually exposed to intensely emotional experiences. Advances in medical technology make some medical decisions tortuously complex and heavy with responsibility. Recently a young woman was brought into the hospital with critical brain damage from a car accident. The physician decided to do emergency cranial surgery and sustain her life by means of respirators and temperature maintenance devices. Much effort was expended to save her life.

After two weeks with no signs of recovery, he decided to discontinue the support mechanisms which had been sustaining her life. She died within an hour. The physician had discussed his decision at some length with colleagues. Nevertheless, when the patient died, and he sensed the deep bereavement of the family, he experienced some grief himself. In speaking with the chaplain about it, he shared some of his sense of loss and also the intense loneliness he experiences inevitably in some medical decisions.

Ministry in the hospital is the responsibility and sometimes the need of the community of hospital staff. The chaplain of necessity is expected to be a specialist in the ministry and may be the only person who can fulfill some sacramental ministerial functions. But the ministry of relationships and service is exercised by all. In every institution there are persons who gladly recognize this. They are ready to serve and eager to serve well. They have been known at times to minister also to the chaplains.

XI

THE HOSPITAL CHAPLAIN AND THE PARISH PASTOR

LAWRENCE E. HOLST

"What difference has your hospital made in the health of the community you serve?"
"Is a disease-oriented hospital the most effective method of dealing with the health problems of your community?"
"What has your hospital done to prevent illness and to contribute to a sense of wholeness in your community?"

THESE were some disturbing questions raised 12,000 miles from Lutheran General Hospital, Park Ridge, Illinois, at a conference on The Healing Ministry of the Church in 1970 in Limuru, Kenya, East Africa, under the sponsorship of the Protestant Churches Medical Association, Nairobi, Kenya, and the Lutheran Institute of Human Ecology, U.S.A.

The questions, of course, were directed at mission hospitals in the underdeveloped countries of Africa. But were they? Upon deeper reflection the questions were just as relevant for hospitals in highly-developed United States.

There is always the temptation for a sophisticated hospital with its armamentarium of technological skills and instruments to become encased. It is comfortable and safe.

But it seems that a mission hospital in Tanzania or in the United States must do more than refine its techniques and wait for needy, hurting and mobile people to come to its doors for treatment. It would seem, rather, that it must move outside its walls to explore the causes of health as well as of illness; that it must struggle with the tension between the clinical pathology of individuals confined to its care and the health concerns of the community.

What is at stake here is a concept of health, as well as of task. If

105

one's concept of health is seen in finite, immediate and functional terms, e.g. the absence of disease, a state in which all defects are eliminated and specific pain is reduced, then undoubtedly the production of this kind of health ought to be the exclusive province of the hospital. Where else can pain be so immediately relieved, disease so effectively cured and one's functional capacities so completely restored?

But if one thinks of health in other terms, such as relational brokeness and reconciliation, in which the experiencing of acceptance by God, others and self is crucial. If one thinks of health not alone as functional perfection, but as a quality of life in which one accepts the limitations of his humanity and lives creatively within them; in which one sees all of life – its deterioration, old age, pain, guilt, despair and death – belonging to God. If one sees health in these larger and deeper ways, then one immediately recognizes that hospital-centered medicine cannot exclusively produce healing. The hospital, to be sure, is a central base and makes its enormous contribution to the production of health; but healing can never be the prerogative of the hospital alone. Its efforts rely upon other health-producing forces within the community.

As a hospital chaplain begins to explore health-producing forces in the community, he is drawn immediately to the local parish and its pastors. Not that these are the only forces (or in some cases even the best), but by training, experience and background the hospital chaplain has an affinity for this sector of community.

HOSPITAL CHAPLAIN VERSUS PARISH PASTOR

Despite this natural affinity, there has often been sharp tension between the hospital chaplain and the parish pastor. As with most tension, much of it has resulted from misunderstanding.

The parish pastor has often felt that the hospital chaplain has forfeited his religious birthright for an assortment of psychological skills which impede his "real ministry to people." Further, he feels that the hospital chaplain over-utilizes "the incarnational model" of ministry with its strong thrust upon relationship, nonverbal communication, feelings and self-understanding and under-utilizes the traditional pastoral resources of prayer, Scripture-reading and the sacraments of Holy Communion.

Part of this feeling is the failure of the parish pastor to realize the context of the hospital chaplain's functioning. Unlike the parish pastor, the hospital chaplain is working essentially with persons he has never met before hospitalization, and with many who do not accord him the pastoral authority which parishioners give their pastor. The chaplain has a universal character to his ministry in that he works with all persons whatever creed or none and encounters them in their crises. What he can immediately share with patients is a participation in their human anguish, but not always in their religious structures, since it will take time to discover what those are. Much of his work is extemporaneous and informal, and personal relationship is the absolute essential for his work.

Since the patient has usually never met the chaplain before, he is apt to trust him only as that chaplain is able to communicate understanding, sensitivity and acceptance, as someone easy to talk to. Coming into the room unannounced and uninvited − as the hospital chaplain often does − it is imperative that these human qualities of empathy and concern be communicated in initiating the relationship. As once observed, "It is the chaplain's humanity, the kind of person he is, that patients and staff look for."

Given this context, it is natural that a hospital chaplain will more immediately utilize his "interpersonal skills" than "the traditional pastoral resources" in his hospital ministry.

Of course this is not to imply that a hospital chaplain never, or even seldom prays, reads Scripture or administers the Sacrament with patients he visits. He does them all as the realtionship is established and the needs for them on the part of individual patients become clarified. (Nor, of course, does this imply that parish pastors are bereft of "interpersonal skills".)

There is, however, a sense in which the hospital chaplain does feel that the parish pastor over-utilizes pastoral rituals and does not often enough take the time or effort to encounter the patient at the "gut level" of his current concerns. But what the hospital chaplain at times fails to realize is that the parish pastor has a prior relationship with most of the persons he visits in the hospital.

Therefore for him it is not a matter of initiating a new relationship, but rather creating out of a general and prior relationship a temporary and special relationship growing out of the temporary and special circumstances of illness. Also, in most instances, the parish pastor knows something of the feelings, attitudes, values and religious structures of his parishioner-patient, who is accustomed to seeing his pastor active in certain religious rituals, such as conducting worship, preaching, praying and distributing the elements of Holy Communion. Therefore it is natural that the parishioner-patient will expect that his pastor will exercise his authority in similar ways in the sick room. This is one of the enormous gifts the parish pastor can bring into the hospital. Through the familiarity of his own person (never to be underestimated) and through the utilization of familiar rituals, the parish pastor in the matter of moments is able to bring structure and order by way of familiar sights, sounds, smells, colors and action into the often chaotic, disintegrating effects of pain. In other words, the parish pastor has a history of formal and informal, professional and personal interaction with the parishioner-patient which can now be immediately drawn upon and utilized.

This is not to say that the parish pastor's use of formal rituals may not at times be contrived ways to avoid deeper involvements in the patient's feelings at the moment, to maintain a safe "ritualized distance"; but it is to recognize, as hospital chaplains sometimes fail to do, that a parish pastor's familiarity with the parishioner-patient often enables him to move more immediately and deeply into the "gut issues" of his experience.

Along with some of these misunderstandings, a part of the tension between the hospital chaplain and parish pastor is a result of each seeing some of his own limitations in the other.

There are times when the hospital chaplain yearns for the redemptive support of a parish, a solid core of people committed to him and to his work. (To be sure, the hospital community meets many of these personal needs for support, but it never fully duplicates that most unique and peculiar bond between a community of believers and its "called pastor." In that covenant there are solemn claims and allegiances not elsewhere found.)

He also feels the lack of the more traditional pastoral public functioning since worship services are generally poorly attended in hospitals. Much of his work is personal in nature and beyond the scrutiny and recognition of others.

He also envies the prior relationships, the "pastoral contracts," the parish pastor has with many of his parishioners he visits in the hospital. Day after day the hospital chaplain starts from scratch, makes initial calls upon patients, few of whom seek him out, and fewer of whom initially are able to articulate a present difficulty or to consciously seek help from him. The chaplain realizes that the utilization of his person and skill will depend upon his initiative and availability.

Most hospital patients will only respond to the stimulus of the chaplain's visit. Hence the chaplain often covets the "contract" the parish pastor has with his parishioners "to visit the sick and to comfort the dying." His place and role in their lives is openly prescribed.

Much of the hospital chaplain's work is not as definable nor as measurable as other professional colleagues on the staff who have tissue committees, laboratories, x-ray, and tests of every kind to evaluate need and therapeutic progress. At times the chaplain yearns for some of the tangible measures the parish pastor has of his work: budgets, membership growth, worship attendance, the maturing of persons in crises and the establishment of families, all of which are, in part, evidences of his ministry.

Furthermore, the hospital chaplain feels limited by his confinement to the parenthesis of illness: he realizes that he sees only a fraction of a person's life. He has not seen the long struggle leading to admission into the hospital, and he will not see the restoration into community again. His is "an episodic ministry," and he often longs for the opportunity to see his work "completed," to have a more balanced or fuller ministry.

THE PARISH PASTOR'S LIMITATIONS

The parish pastor too senses some of his personal and situational limitations as he looks at the hospital chaplain.

While the chaplain lacks a familiarity with the patient upon admission, the parish pastor lacks a familiarity with the hospital.

Unfamiliar with the routines and personnel of the hospital, the parish pastor often feels insecure in it. This is not his world, he has little status or power there, and his entrance into and exit from the place is often hasty. He envies the chaplain's almost unlimited accessibility to the hospital's "inner sanctums," his personal acquaintance with physicians and nurses and his familiarity with medical terminology.

Also, at times he feels that his prior relationship with his parishioner-patients is overrated. Being exposed to persons in the normal routines of life often means very little when confronted by the deeper needs that are unmasked in these same persons by the crisis of illness. The parish pastor tends to feel that those in the hospital see more of the real stuff of life than he does in the routines of parish life. It is true that in confronting illness one is exposed more dynamically to man's struggle for meaning in life. Such crises unlock the secrets of one's fundamental struggle for existence, his basic attitudes toward life, his values, conflicts and purposes. Consequently, though he is visiting with a person in the hospital whom he knew outside the hospital, the parish pastor often discovers that the experience of illness has almost rendered this person a stranger to him.

Many social adjustments in life are based upon the repression of feelings. Disease reduces energy available to the patient, including that needed for the function of repression. Primitive tendencies suddenly surge to the surface: strong feelings of rebellion, resentments that have been smoldering for years, irritability and depression. It may prove to be perplexing and embarrassing to these two persons who knew each other so well before the crisis, or at least thought they did.

The parish pastor also feels less accessibility to his parishioner-patient during the period of hospitalization. Unlike the chaplain who is in the hospital all day, the parish pastor is able to spend only a small portion of his day there. The time he has chosen to make a visit may not be a good one for his parishioner, but the pastor cannot easily return later that day at a better time. Patients have their "waves of pain," their periods of alertness and their moments of openness. But the parish pastor's visitation schedule may not always coincide with these fluctuations.

He often yearns for the flexible accessibility to patients that the hospital chaplain enjoys who can visit two or three times a day and more accurately gear his visits to the physical and emotional availability of the patient.

Finally, the parish pastor often feels the lack of specific training in sick visitation. He is a generalist and has a number of broadly-defined functions in the parish, which includes visiting and comforting the sick. But he cannot begin to give to that function the time, energy and special preparation that the hospital chaplain can give to it.

If he has not had clinical pastoral education, the parish pastor may feel that he lacks a professional preciseness in the art of sick visitation, and that he lacks the internalized criteria by which he can measure the effectiveness of his approach. If he is the only pastor on the parish staff, he may not have access to adequate feedback that will enable him to grow in his interpersonal effectiveness. In a typical parish setting, the pastor's primary feedback comes in areas where laymen feel equipped to give it: in administration, finances, the pastor's personal appearance and conduct in the community. Rarely does the parish pastor have an opportunity — and in some cases a willingness — to submit his pastoral care of individuals to the scrutiny of his colleagues or specialists in the field. He frequently covets the chaplain's training for his task. This training included individual supervision and group feedback to his personal style; and developing skills in ministering. In addition, where the chaplain is open and willing, he can seek and get honest evaluations on the effectiveness of his work from persons in other professions who have skills in the art of communication and interpersonal relationships.

As a generalist who is called upon to do many things in a parish, the pastor often covets the hospital chaplain's specificity of function and the specialized training that has prepared him for that function.

Because of these misunderstandings, and the limitations each symbolizes in the other, there has been tension between the hospital chaplain and the parish pastor.

HOSPITAL CHAPLAIN AND THE
PARISH PASTOR AS A UNIT

As these tensions ease, each profession is better able to recognize what it can give and receive from the other. For each can enhance the other, and each can supplement the other in fostering a healthier community.

Lutheran General Hospital has attempted a program of Information-Education-Collaboration, which has contributed toward a better relationship between the chaplain and the parish pastor in the hospital.

Information

When a patient is admitted to the hospital, he is asked his religious affiliation, the name of the parish he attends and whether he would want his pastor notified of his hospitalization. Some 35 to 40 percent of patients give this consent. The chaplain in his initial visit upon the patient may also inquire about his church affiliation and pastor notification.

Where permission is granted, a secretary makes a phone call to the parish. The pastor may be notified on the day of admission, or at least by the second day of hospitalization.

The secretary notifies the parish pastor of the patient's name, date of admission, room number and the chaplain assigned to that parishioner-patient's floor.

This secretary-receptionist sits in an office just off the main lobby (very valuable real estate when one considers the high demands for space in hospitals today) which is set aside for parish pastors. This full-time salaried secretary occupies her entire five-day week to the service of visiting parish pastors.

Aside from the daily telephone calls to parishes (about 40 per day), she maintains an up-to-date card file of all patients according to religious denomination and suburb. The card includes the name and address of the patient, room number, admitting physician's name, nearest of kin and religious denomination if one is given. This card is provided this office by the Admitting Department.

Pastors making visits in the hospital are able to look over the card file and pick up names of parishioners who did not choose to have them notified (sometimes because of misunderstanding or slip-ups in the admitting procedure, sometimes because the parishioner did not want "to bother the pastor" and sometimes because the anticipated hospitalization was to be two or three days).

The hospital's position is that it is not a violation of confidentiality to have a patient list available to parish pastors who come into the hospital. However, a pastor is not notified against the wishes of a patient.

In this office the pastor has a place to sit, to hang his hat, to receive phone messages and to feel that he has a place in the vast, complicated world of the hospital.

The visiting pastor is also given a name tag so that he can be properly identified by the staff. This is particularly important if the visiting pastor does not wear a clerical collar.

In the event of a crisis within the hospitalization, including death, the pastor may also be called.

This relatively simple program of information – duplicated in many hospitals – has done much to foster good relations and to communicate to the parish pastor a sense of belonging. A hospital that is willing to devote strategic space and secretarial help to the visiting clergy is communicating acceptance.

Education

Through the years, the Department of Pastoral Care has offered a variety of educational programs for the parish pastor. Some have been intended to introduce the pastor to the hospital, others have been an attempt to share skills and insights in the care of the sick.

A very helpful orientation program has been offered to familiarize the pastor with hospital routine and terminology. It runs for 10 consecutive weeks, one morning a week. The chaplain serves as the coordinator, but other professionals are mobilized as teaching resources.

The program is designed as follows:

Week 1 – The Patient Is Admitted
Physician discusses his use of diagnostic facilities in the hospital.

Visit to hospital laboratory (guided by pathologist), and X-ray (guided by radiologist).
Chaplain discusses initial patient reactions to hospital admission.

Week 2 – The Obstetrical Patient

Physician shows film on a birth; discusses gynecologic problems.
Chaplain discusses reactions to pregnancy, spontaneous abortion, stillbirth and hysterectomy.

Week 3 – The Pediatric Patient

Physician discusses dynamics of illness in child.
Visit to pediatric floor and meeting with head nurse.
Chaplain discusses parent-child relations in illness.

Week 4 – The Surgical Patient

Surgeon discusses role of surgery in treatment of disease.
Anesthesiologist discusses his role in surgery with tour of the surgical area.
Chaplain discusses pre-op visit.

Week 5 – The Medical Patient

Physician discusses internal medical problems.
Tour of medical floor, with nurse identifying by name and function common hospital apparatus.
Chaplain discusses meaning of illness.

Week 6 – The Orthopedic Patient

Orthopedic surgeon discusses field of orthopedics.
Nurse describes and demonstrates apparatus on orthopedic floor.
Chaplain discusses reactions and needs of orthopedic patient.

Week 7 – The Coronary Patient

Physician describes coronary disease.
Chaplain discusses emotional needs of coronary patient and describes group approach to care of coronary patient.

Week 8 – The Cancer Patient

Physician discusses various types of cancer.
Panel discussion on the role with the dying – the physician, nurse and chaplain.

Week 9 – The Dying Patient

Physician discusses physical and emotional needs of the dying.
Chaplain discusses the stages of grief.

Week 10 – The Administration of Hospital

Administrator discusses administration of hospital: includes organizational chart of hospital, financing and relations with community.

The program, usually limited to eight to ten pastors, has contributed toward overcoming some of the unfamiliarity about hospitals felt by many pastors. It has introduced them to certain areas of the hospital, helped to identify terms, acquainted them with some of the people who occupy important positions there and has broadened their appreciation of the complexities and problems in running hospitals today.

Many other educational programs have been offered which have moved at greater depth in discussing the human personality, how it develops, what it needs, how it copes with crisis.

It has always been a defined task of the Pastoral Care Department to teach. There has been the recognition that the hospital has within its walls a reservoir of skilled, highly-trained professional persons whose sole task should not be the cure of the sick, but who should also share their knowledge with others in the community. These have included physicians, psychiatrists, clinical psychologists, social workers, nurses, laboratory technicians and administrators.

Aside from the value accrued for the parish pastor, it has been the experience that it is good for the hospital to teach. It has been an extremely worthwhile experience for a physician to conceptualize his ideas on the need of the dying or for an anesthesiologist to identify the psychological concerns of the preoperative patient.

Furthermore, it has been good to bring parish pastors together with other professional persons. It is easy for a parish pastor to maintain an active ministry, but to have little to do directly with a physician, a pathologist, a radiologist or a clinical psychologist. With little contact, it is easy for stereotypes to develop.

It has been a refreshing experience for parish pastors to discover that not every physician is irreligious or coldly scientific. It has been equally enlightening for physicians to discover that ministers do more than pontificate, or condemn or hide behind meaningless platitudes.

The bringing together through education has been a mutually growing experience. While it is true that on the surface the pastor comes in as a "student" and the physician as a "teacher," roles often became reversed in the discussions that ensue.

Collaboration

Probably the most valuable experience has been when the parish pastor and the hospital chaplain have collaborated in their care of the sick. This has been done formally in case conferences, where the pastor is frequently invited to participate when the patient under discussion is his parishioner. It also happens informally on the wards as they meet together to share their concerns and skills about a particular patient. Each brings something unique to the scene.

The parish pastor brings with him a larger context in which to view the illness and react to the onset of symptoms; he has seen the involvement of family, job and environment in illness.

The chaplain and the hospital may tend to see illness as more episodic, as a parenthesis in the life of that person. They floodlight that parenthesis, that episode, and by so doing are able to see more deeply into the personality structure, the intrapersonal conflicts, the raw needs, the basic values of that person as they are unmasked by illness.

Yet each view – the broader and the more intensive – contributes toward a fuller perspective of the person who is ill.

The parish pastor may be the only professional person who is dynamically involved on each side of that parenthesis. He may be the key person in mobilizing family members, employer and neighbors to play constructive roles in the restoration to health of that person. He may be a key person in mobilizing concerned people within the fellowship of the congregation to render some of the tangible services required by the ill: cooking, baby-sitting, transportation to and from the hospital.

The parish pastor serves as a constant reminder to the hospital that illness is a dynamic series of events which happen largely outside of the hospital, and that much of the restoration to health will also take place largely outside of the hospital with the help of the patient's family and larger community.

Together with these unique exposures to the life of the ill person the hospital chaplain and the parish pastor can offer considerable to persons if they continue to find ways to creatively collaborate.

XII

A COMMUNITY PASTORAL
COUNSELING CENTER

LAWRENCE E. HOLST

COLLABORATION between the hospital and the local parish becomes imperative if the following propositions are accepted.

1. Health and illness may be more broadly and deeply defined as personal brokenness and reconciliation with God, self and others rather than more narrowly and finitely as the capacity or incapacity to function physically.
2. Since many turn to the hospital seeking only relief from pain and functional restoration, it is the task of the hospital to make available its vast technical resources to meet those needs with competence and compassion but always with the hope that health and healing will be seen in the broader, ultimate dimensions.
3. When health and healing are seen in the above terms, then the hospital plays a vital but fractional role in the total healing of man, while the community plays a larger role.
4. The parish is a vital sector of that total community where the healing or growth of persons is a goal (for all) and a reality (for many).
5. To continue to effect this growth role it is crucial that the parish mobilize its personal resources to maintain a redemptive fellowship that fosters the healing and growth of persons.
6. With these common concerns and with a diversity of resources and settings, it is imperative that the hospital — particularly a church-related hospital — and local parish collaborate to meet the desperate needs of a broken society.

With these ideas in mind, Lutheran General Hospital and 14 local parishes formed the Community Pastoral Counseling and Consultation Center in 1971. It was formed with four basic purposes:

1. To provide a resource of skilled pastoral counseling for troubled

people in the community, combining the best of religious and psychological insights.

2. To provide a consultative service for pastors who are seeking more effective ways to contribute to the growth of persons in his parish.

3. To explore ways in which mature and concerned members of a parish might be more effectively mobilized and utilized to strengthen the interpersonal milieu of their parish

4. To develop a training center under the auspices of the American Association of Pastoral Counselors for those clergy who want to specialize in pastoral counseling.

The administration and financing of the center are conducted jointly by the member-parishes and the Department of Pastoral Care of the hospital.* To join the center, a parish contributes $1000 annually to it and provides a representative to the advisory council which is responsible for the policies, directions and operation of the center. The hospital administration and the medical staff are also represented.

Each counselee is expected to pay for services rendered according to his financial capability. (The average fee at the center has been $16 per session). There is also a charge for the intake work-up and staffing.

During its first year of operation 314 persons were counseled at the center for a total of 1,600 hours. Of these 203 were referred by parish pastors.

Personnel in 1971 includes three pastoral counselors who are ordained clergymen, have had graduate training in pastoral counseling and are members of the American Association of Pastoral Counselors or the American Association of Marriage and Family Counselors. They are on an annual salary.

A psychiatrist is retained as a consultant and participates in all intake staffings and makes recommendations on treatment or disposition. He does no therapy at the center and accepts no referrals from it into his private practice. A family and group therapy consultant has also been engaged.

A clinical psychologist is available for psychological testing interpretation when requested by the pastoral counselor. He too

---

*The structure of the center is largely patterened after the Greater Washington Pastoral Counseling Center, Washington, D.C.

does no therapy at the center, nor does he accept referrals from it into his private practice.

A secretary-bookkeeper has responsibility for scheduling appointments, keeping records, sending out statements and maintaining files.

BACKGROUND OF THE CENTER

Perhaps the best way to describe the function of this collaborative effort between the hospital and the parish is to re-define and elaborate upon its purposes.

  1. *To provide a resource of skilled pastoral counseling for troubled persons in the community, combining the best of religious and modern psychological insights.*

Man is created for relationship with God, self and others. This is the most profound description of man there is. These relationships are inter-dependent and inter-related. It is highly doubtful that one can have a healthy, mature and satisfying relationship with God when his interpersonal relationships are characterized by aloofness and superficiality. Likewise, if one does not see himself as a worthwhile and acceptable human being, it is highly unlikely that he will believe with any depth or conviction that God finds him so.

The church's task is the same today as it has always been: to increase man's love for God, self and neighbor.

In this age we undoubtedly realize more clearly than ever that man's basic needs in life (defined here as trust, safety, a sense of belonging, self-acceptance, autonomy, identity and meaning) are not inborn, they are learned. They are learned or experienced through relationships with loving, understanding and emotionally generous persons, particularly in the formative years of development.

Out of these relationships one begins to develop feelings about himself ("I am worthy or unworthy, important or unimportant"); about others ("They are predictable or unpredictable, trustworthy or untrustworthy"); and about authority ("They are arbitrary or flexible, demanding and demeaning or affirming"). Through these relationships one's attitudes toward himself, God, and the world around him develop.

This is not to suggest that all of one's interpersonal experiences are totally good and healthy or totally bad and destructive. They are a blend of both since they are communicated by human beings who are a blend of both. But certain themes do predominate, depending upon the messages sent to, and received by, the individual.

Human relationships predispose one to respond to self and to others. In other words, one responds against a background of feelings, personality structure and interpersonal experiences. For some their human ties have been so poor and damaging that they are severely blocked in terms of responding to love or acceptance in a trusting way. Such persons usually cannot break out of their web alone, but need help from the sphere where the unsatisfactory relationships were fostered, namely, with another human being. When another human can help him to feel understood, accepted, and worthwhile, it will greatly enhance his capacity to trust and to commit himself to God, self and others.

This in no way suggests that God is only a human projection, or that His love is not prior to or greater than any human love. It affirms that one's perceptions of God, self and others come largely through human encounters.

For too long the church has relied too heavily upon verbal proclamations of the Gospel without a similar concern for the interpersonal climate of its fellowship. Words, formulations and verbal pronouncements about the faith have an important place in the life and worship of God's people. But words are only symbols. And symbols depend upon the experiences and associations of the beholder. Interpretations become highly subjective.

Since most Christian symbols are relational in nature, the association persons bring to them will closely parallel the interpersonal relationships they have experienced or are now experiencing. These become the associations persons bring to those symbols. While one's own personal meanings or interpretations may not accurately represent what the church is attempting to teach doctrinally through those symbols, nevertheless that is the "reality" he brings to them and takes from them. That "reality" will change not alone by more precise teachings of church dogma (though that is part of it), but by the church helping to foster an interpersonal milieu for its members which exemplifies the truth it is proclaiming at a dynamic and relational level.

For ages the church has said that as one's relationship with God is right so will he be right with the world. Perhaps there is so much truth to that statement that one can miss the error. For it would seem equally true that as one becomes right with his fellow so he will be right with God. Either of those statements taken by itself, without the other, is a serious distortion.

If what has been said is true, then the task of the local parish is to help to provide that interpersonal climate in which the enduring truths of the Gospel can be embodied in tangible, concrete relationships.

To help the parish do this is a basic aim of the center. However, there are those who are confronted by crises, whose capacity to cope is severely limited and whose lives have become warped by internal conflicts and emotional entanglements. They need special help from one who has had special training in understanding human conflict and its resolution. This is a particular role of the center.

WHO USES THE CENTER

All kinds of people come to the center, but most of them come from parishes in the area who are seeking to work out their problems through the ministry of the church. The following are some of the problems or situational dilemmas that bring people to the center:

Marriage or family problems, parent-child relationships

Problems in one's personal life e.g. anxiety, doubt, feelings of failure, a sense of unhappiness or a lack of fulfillment

Problems of work relationships

Adolescents facing difficulties in school, or in social or religious life

Premarital counseling

Problems of conscience, either guilt feelings about behavior or a conflict of values

Persons feeling that life has lost its meaning or significance

Emotional and spiritual problems related to physical illness

Persons suffering from a prolonged bereavement or a sense of personal loss

Persons with religious problems which have not been resolved through the usual religious approaches

Problems of aging and retirement.

When an appointment is made a counselor does an intake work-up which includes an assessment of the presenting problem, a brief life history and an analysis of material in terms of the personality of that individual. When the intake work-up is completed (probably in two to four sessions), a staff meeting is held. In addition to the staff counselors and the center's psychiatric consultant, the referring person (usually a parish pastor) is invited to attend this staff meeting with the counselee's permission. At the conference, decisions are made concerning the best way to help this individual. When present, the parish pastor takes an active role in the meeting by sharing his broader contact with the counselee.

After the staff conference, an individual session is held between the staff counselor and the counselee to discuss the recommendations of the center. The counselee is free to accept, reject or attempt to modify those recommendations.

If a referral is then made outside the center, the pastoral counselor personally helps to complete the referral.

In either case, the parish pastor is aware of the center's recommendation and the counselee's decision and can then minister accordingly. At the intake conference considerable time is spent discussing the role of the parish pastor with this person and family, whether they are to remain in counseling at the center or are referred to another therapist or agency.

If the counselee continues in counseling at the center, then the pastoral counselor is responsible for keeping adequate records and staying in touch with the parish pastor and the family as indicated. Brief staff conferences are held periodically to evaluate growth and progress.

At the termination of counseling, for whatever reason, an adequate record is made of the circumstances surrounding the termination and the referring person is informed of it.

REFERRAL REASONS

Pastors will most commonly refer to the center those individuals in his parish whom he feels are struggling with problems that are beyond his time or training or where he feels that his general, ongoing pastoral relationship does not lend itself to the specific, more temporary and intensive kind of pastoral counseling relationship.

Any of these reasons are legitimate. Time is a factor in the parish pastor's schedule. His attention to organizational and administrative matters, preaching, teaching, evangelism, sickness and bereavement ministry often allows little time for intensive, long-term individual counseling. The center offers him an opportunity to broaden the ministry of his church by referring those persons whose conflicts will require more time than he can give. This is not a "cop-out" for the parish pastor. This is part of the reality of a tremendously demanding time schedule.

Lack of training is also a legitimate cause for referral. The general nature of the pastorate often does not permit the parish pastor to prepare adequately for all of his individual tasks. He may have little preparation for individual counseling beyond courses at the seminary and occasional reading and seminars. Many parish pastors agree to meet with troubled parishioners for a set number of interviews (between three to five) and if some resolutions have not occurred by then, this is indication for a referral. To admit one's limitations might be the better part of wisdom and compassion as well.

The ongoing character of relationships in the parish is also at times an indication for referral. The pastor's accessibility to people in the total context of their lives may make it extremely difficult for him to maintain the objectivity and exclusiveness that a counseling relationship demands. To be a preacher, teacher, neighbor, friend, board adviser, fellow-Kiwanian, co-worker on the building committee and stewardship drive may enhance the pastor's capacity to render total pastoral care, but might pose obstacles to an intensive pastoral counseling relationship. On occasion it is prudent for the parish pastor to refer those from his congregation who need counseling help to another who can enjoy the "luxury" of a more limited relationship with that individual. Parishes which are part of the center are discovering that when its troubled people receive needed help with their personal struggles, they are better able to enter into mature, mutually satisfying relationships with others in that parish. As such efforts multiply, these parishes are experiencing a slow transformation in the interpersonal climate of their fellowship and they are increasingly becoming places where reconciliation can be an experienced reality.

2. *To provide a consultation service for pastors who are seeking more effective ways to contribute to the growth of persons in their parishes.*

The center in no way attempts to displace the parish pastor as one who facilitates growth in persons. It seeks to enhance that facilitation whenever it can.

Every parish pastor is involved in a variety of relationships and functions which offer the potential for human growth. The diversity of his role is both its attraction and frustration.

Not all of the help the pastor offers to his people can, or necessarily should, be neatly structured into formal counseling relationships, as is possible in the center. Much of his work is extemporaneous and informal, encountering people where he meets them: after Sunday worship, at board and committee meetings, in the hospital room, in the coffee shop, on the post-office steps or at the bank. The tremendous accessibility he has to people and they have to him demands flexibility on the pastor's part, to say nothing of endurance.

This broad exposure to people brings the pastor into contact with a wide spectrum of personalities, with a similarly wide spectrum of problems and needs. He has to be especially sensitive to the "messages" of people who may be seeking help in unconscious and indeliberate ways. This is not a plea for the parish pastor to be constantly vigilant for psychopathology in his congregation, but to recognize that many "incidental encounters" do contain "a plea for help." Or, if not a plea for help, many of these encounters contain the potential for growth.

Unlike the counseling center, where a pastoral counselor and a counselee can "contract" to deal with acknowledged problems (to meet at a certain hour each week in a designated place and to reach certain hoped-for resolutions), the parish pastor must meet people where they are and often on their terms. The counseling center staff is available as a consultant to the parish pastor to help him strengthen his interpersonal effectiveness not only in his formal counseling relationships, but also in the more numerous informal, extemporaneous relationships.

This does not presume a parish expertise at the center. Its expertise (and the real help it can offer parish pastors) is in the area of human personality: how it develops, functions, copes and communicates in verbal and nonverbal ways. How the pastor will utilize this kind of understanding in his many and varied parish relationships is up to him.

The really important thing is that in the center the parish pastor has a trusted colleague with whom he can share certain dimensions of his ministry for feedback, impressions and possible recommendations. In many ways ministers have been the most closed of all the professions about the deeply personal and relational issues of their ministry. Certain facts about worship attendance, membership statistics, even the pastor's salary and car allowance have always been public domain. But how pastors relate to persons, how they feel about what they are doing, how they respond to needs — these often remain secret. The price ministers pay for this secrecy is often a lack of growth and considerable loneliness.

Hopefully, the center provides a place where the parish pastor can more fully explore the needs of people, as well as his own needs and feelings in responding to those needs. The center does not view this as psychotherapy for the pastor, but as a means of professional collaboration and personal growth. The most important instrument the pastor has in his work is his own person; how that person grows, develops and deepens in its sensitivities becomes an important determinant of effectiveness. The growth of the pastor through consultation is a basic aim of the center.

The parish pastor has a formal and informal entree into the consultative services of the center. He may enroll in the center's course in pastoral counseling. This includes a one-and-one-half hour weekly didatic session on personality development, psychodynamics and psychopathology, plus an hour of individual supervision for his parish counseling with a staff counselor. This course runs for nine months. Tuition is charged.

Or, any parish pastor may make periodic arrangements to discuss specific counseling problems. He may contact the center in person or by telephone.

> *3. To explore ways in which mature and concerned members of a parish might be more effectively mobilized and utilized to strengthen the interpersonal milieu of their parishes.*

At present this is more a dream than a reality at the center. Down the road it is hoped that the center and the parishes together might find more creative ways in which persons can encounter one another and their communities.

Many books and articles have been written about the "uniqueness of pastoral counseling." The most significant uniqueness is "the representative character" of parish pastoral counseling. The pastor represents a community of concerned people, an established fellowship. No other helping profession has a comparable supportive fellowship so immediately available as does the parish pastor. To arouse and mobilize that fellowship to more meaningfully meet the needs of a lonely, depersonalized society is the single most urgent challenge facing the church today. To fail at this is to fail to meet man at his level of deepest need.

Present plans call for the center to bring on its staff counselors with particular skills in mobilizing parish manpower to more effectively meet the serious interpersonal needs of our age. When done, this could represent yet the most effective collaboration between the hospital and the parish: to help persons become better ministers to one another.

XIII

THE RELIGIOUS INTERVIEW
AS A METHOD
FOR TEACHING PSYCHODYNAMICS

A Research Project in
Pastoral Counseling

E. ALAN RICHARDSON

INSTRUCTORS in the field of pastoral counseling have for years struggled with a linguistic dilemma: how to teach the concepts and skills of diagnosis and psychodynamics to students who are professionally educated in the language of theology. This chapter describes a research project which tries to deal with this dilemma in a different way.

The only way to teach diagnosis and psychodynamics is to establish contact with the discoveries in the behavioral sciences through their language, their nosology, their dynamic formulations and their therapeutic methods. The initial effect which this has had upon students in pastoral counseling has been to engender anxiety and varying degrees of confusion. To be confronted with a new language is a threat to whatever level of personal integration one has achieved. Some students react to this threat by avoidance of the issues or by introjecting the concepts without integrating them with what they already know. Others react by abandoning the theological community and immersing themselves in the new "religion" of psychotherapy. (This, unfortunately, often occurs with the better students.) Still others try to hold both systems of thought in tension in the hope of eventually integrating them.

What this project attempts to do is to provide a linguistic bridge between the teaching of theology and the teaching of psychotherapy. This bridge is the religious interview. The religious interview is a traditional part of pastoral care. Usually informal and unstructured, it has been a *modus operandi* for pastors to come to know their people in a personal way. This study has attempted to move into a semistructured interview of specific religious questions and then to examine the answers from the perspective of psychodynamics.

These interviews were conducted by one-year residents in the Department of Pastoral Care at Lutheran General Hospital. Those interviewed were hospitalized patients being treated in the departments of psychiatry or medicine. Before discussing at length the methodology involved, there is a need to place this study in its historical perspective and to spell out certain methodological assumptions upon which this study is based.

This study views religion from its functional perspective, i.e. what particular function a religious idea serves in the preservation and enhancement of an individual life. This is in contrast to those studies of religion which see it from its dogmatic perspective. The functional concept of religion is development which grew out of discoveries in the eighteenth and nineteenth centuries in biology and psychology. It also has antecedents in the rise of secular thought and skepticism in England and France in the seventeenth century.

The anthropologist Malinowski first developed the concept of functional analysis and saw all social systems, including religion, as having specific functional, adaptive value for the preservation of the individual in a society. Radcliffe-Brown developed this concept further in maintaining that practices of society are functional for the preservation of the total social life and for the maintenance of a unified social system. Radcliffe-Brown's utilitarian theory saw positive social value in all religious rituals.

Freud viewed religion from the psychological perspective. He saw in religious ideas and institutions an example of collective fantasies which have great adaptive value and which spring from the same intrapsychic sources as do those of isolated individuals.

Eliade developed a concept of "hierophanies" to describe the myriad experiences of the sacred in primitive societies and attempts to trace the forms these experiences have taken across the earth and throughout time.

Paul Ricoeur, a phenomenological philosopher, has attempted to bring together the methodologies of Freud and Eliade in a way which combines both the demystifying analysis of Freud and the phenomenological study of the power of mystical experience for man.

All of these approaches, whether they see religion as authentic or neurotic, sacred or profane, view it from the functional point of view. This study is an extension of this method of investigation. The religious ideas of patients from the functional point of view have been studied and have seen these ideas as having great adaptive value and mystical power.

ASSUMPTIONS

There are a number of underlying assumptions which the research project believed true and upon which we proceeded. The first of these is that the language of religion is functional as well as dogmatic. It was assumed that specific religious ideas become important to a person because they help that person cope with a particular life situation and that these ideas will vary in importance as situations in life change.

Second, the study assumed the perspectival nature of truth, i.e. that the meaning of "truth" cannot be stated except in reference to the presuppositions of the perspective in which it appears. Truth is contextual and personal.

Third, the study assumed that there is an empirical link between theology and psychology. As seen in the clinical setting, all of the helping professions seek to understand the "living human document" (to use a phrase of Anton Boisen) with the particular tools, skills and presuppositions of that profession.

Fourth, the study assumed that the making of a diagnosis and developing a psychodynamic formulation is a worthwhile and necessary part of adequate pastoral care. (For a full discussion of this thesis, see Edgar Draper, *Psychiatry and Pastoral Care*).

Fifth, it was assumed that the semistructured religious interview is an adequate vehicle for developing a diagnosis and a psychodynamic formulation. This assumption is based on the research done by Draper *et al* and published under the title, *The Diagnostic*

Value of Religious Ideation.

Sixth, the study assumed that individual and group supervision could provide an adequate context in which learning could be facilitated.

Finally, the study assumed that the project was compatible with the overall methods and goals of clinical pastoral education.

THE QUESTIONNAIRE

During the three-year project, two versions of the questionnaire were used. First used was the same questionnaire which the Draper team used in their project. The questionnaire follows:

1. What is your earliest memory of a religious experience or belief?
2. What is your favorite Bible story? Why?
3. What is your favorite Bible verse. Why?
4. Who is your favorite Bible character. Why?
5. What does prayer mean to you? If you pray, what do you pray about?
6. a. What does religion mean to you?
   b. How does God function in your personal life?
7. a. In what way is God meaningful to other people besides yourself?
   b. How is God meaningful to father or mother?
8. What religious idea or concept is most important to you now?
9. What is the most religious act one can perform?
10. What do you consider the greatest sin one could commit?
11. What do you think of evil in the world?
12. What are your ideas of an afterlife?
13. If God could grant you any three wishes, what would they be?

Because of the obvious success of the Draper project, we decided to duplicate his method. The residents were instructed to use the questionnaire as shown above. As we proceeded, we realized that it would work better if the residents were free to cover the questions in their own way and to follow those openings for investigation which patients provided.

At the end of the first year, we decided to revise the questionnaire. It was felt that some of the questions could be made more clearly understood, that some seemed unproductive for our purposes and that other areas needed exploration. After a number of group consultaiton, the following revision was devised:

1. What is your earliest memory of a religious nature?
2. What were your religious beliefs as a child?
3. What is God like to you now?
4. What is your favorite Bible or religious story? Why?
5. What is your favorite Bible verse or religious saying? Why?
6. Who is your favorite Bi ble or religious character? Why?
7. If you pray, what do you pray about? Why?
8. What does religion or your faith mean to you?
9. How do you feel about the church, your clergyman?
10. How is (was) God meaningful to your father and mother?
11. What religious idea is most important to you now?
12. What is the most religious act one can perform?
13. What do you consider the greatest sin one could commit?
14. How do you see God involved in illness?
15. What are your ideas about an afterlife?
16. If God granted you any three wishes, what would they be?

It is probable that further revisions will be made, particularly in the light of spontaneous data supplied by patients. Also we are attempting to develop a short version which can be used where the longer list of questions seems contraindicated (e.g. with cardiac and post-surgical patients.)

The first step in the program with the residents is a pre-testing of them through the religious interview. One of the supervisors interviews each of the one-year residents and makes a psychodynamic evaluation of them prior to their understanding of the projective nature of the questions. This diagnostic work-up is compared with the results of the standard psychological battery of tests which they have already taken. Later, usually in the second quarter, the results are discussed with them, either individually or as a group.

Before the project was begun a meeting was held with the research team and a select group of psychiatrists (internists were later included). The project goals were outlined, and the physicians agreed to allow the residents to interview their patients. They were also asked to submit a diagnostic report on each of their interviewed patients which would be used for correlating the results.

Patients were selected on a random basis. A list of all patients admitted under the care of the cooperating physicians was kept in the pastoral care office. Residents would select a name at random, arrange with the individual patient for an appointment and conduct the interview.

The interviews were conducted either in the patient's room or in one of the consultation rooms on the floor. Each interview was tape recorded in the patient's presence. (In a few isolated instances the interview was rejected because of the tape recorder.)

After the interview, the resident would present the tape for study at his next session of individual supervision. Each resident would work with at least two supervisors over the two quarters. Together they would listen to the tape, discuss significant data and arrive at a tentative diagnosis and a psychodynamic formulation. The diagnostic categories in the *Diagnostic and Statistical Manual of the American Psychiatric Association,* Second Edition, were used. The supervisory session would last from 60 to 90 minutes.

From the tapes which were analyzed, one or two representative tapes were chosen for class presentation, which all residents and supervisors attended. Attention was given to teaching how a diagnostic workup was made from the material and also emphasis was placed on the involvement of the resident, his strengths and his weaknesses.

In both the individual and group supervision, certain didactic steps were followed. In step one the supervisor would demonstrate his own methods for arriving at an understanding of the patients, pointing to the significant material used. Also emphasis was placed on helping the resident develop skill in conducting the interview and helping him deal with his anxieties about the project.

Step two involved a gradual shift of responsibility from the supervisor to the resident as he was continually encouraged to share his thoughts about the patient and to begin to make his own assessment.

Step three, which only has occurred in the second quarter, consists of the resident presenting the tape before the group with little assistance from his supervisor. Step four involved a gradual shift from time spent in arriving at a diagnostic assessment to time spent in discussing alternatives of therapeutic intervention.

CASE SUMMARIES

While it is not possible to adequately discuss in a brief space how the interview is used for teaching, some effort will be made here to give a sampling of two interviews.

Case 1. Patient is a twenty-six-year-old married woman, Roman Catholic. In answer to the question, "What is your earliest memory of a religious nature?" the patient replied, "We used to go to church every Sunday. My sister and I had to go to church by ourselves. For some reason my mother wouldn't go. We couldn't talk in church. I remember that the nun used to push me down, if I talked." To the question "What were your religious beliefs as a child?" she said, "If you obey the ten commandments and are baptized a Catholic, you are saved. No one else was." To the question, "What is God like to you now?" she answered, "I don't know. I don't know where he is. I always was staunch in my beliefs, but somehow, now, I can't accept God. I've never done anything really wrong. Now we're supposed to use birth control pills. It's like a block. It's like God is a barrier. The priest has given me dispensation to use birth control pills, but I don't feel God approves." Her favorite Bible story was, "the ten virgins holding up the candles. It seemed so sweet." Her favorite Bible or religious character is "St. Gerard. He is the patron saint of mothers. I have had six pregnancies in five years. I always threaten to lose them. And I pray to him to help me." When asked what her faith means to her, she said, "I'm not sure now. Before it was a foundation. I'd go to church and feel good. I always brought all of my children to church to prove I had children. But the kids used to show off and then, too, I'd feel guilty because I had the most children. You know, I think I was too proud, that I used my children to impress people." In answer to the question of how God was meaningful to her parents, she replied, "My father was an invalid. He lived in a wheelchair. He died when I was 12. I don't know what he believed. My mother is very religious. She can't understand my feelings now, my doubts. She says, 'I'm praying for you.' " When asked "What is the most religious act a person can perform?" she said, "To lead a good life. To be clean and spotless so that when I die, God will take me to heaven." The greatest sin she felt was, "Like I'm doing now, that I've shut God off. Maybe killing is." To the question, "What are your ideas about an afterlife?" she said, "Heaven is for the good. Hell is for people who did terrible, terrible things."

She was described by the chaplain as having a depressive neurosis in a passive-dependent personality. A second diagnostic choice was a schizo-affective personality of a depressive type. She was seen as having a very primitive psychic structure. Her thinking is at a pre-Oedipal level. She appears to have experienced primary deprivation. What she lacked from her parents, she early transferred to the church, which represented some kind of solidity. Now she appears to have lost her security in the church. Once the mother-church was, if not loving, at least firm and consistent. Now she feels abandoned again. She is angry at the church, her mother and her husband. But because of her fear of abandonment, she has turned the anger inward in the form of depression. Her frequent pregnancies have been both a childlike compliance to the mother-church and a desperate desire to prove her adequacy. Inwardly she feels resentful of her children and their demands. Basically she has a stronger wish to be mothered than to mother.

Case 2. Patient is a 61-year-old man, married, Presbyterian. His earliest memory of a religious nature was as follows: "For the first eight years, I lived in Chicago. I went to the closest church, which was Baptist. It was a Bohemian neighborhood. I wasn't close to anybody. When I was nine, we moved. I went to a Presbyterian church. The Jewish people were overtaking the neighborhood. Then we moved to Cicero. At that time it was mostly truck farmers and the Dutch." In answer to the question, "What is God like to you now?" he said, "I've always wanted more proof. If there is a God, why did I lose my father at an early age? My mother was good and kind. I remember how hard and long she worked on her hands and knees. If there is a God, why would this be tolerated? When I'm in pain and on my back, I turn to God and pray, 'Dear God, please help me.' God comes in front like a big picture window. I attend church on rare occasions. My wife attends church more than I do. There must be a supreme being." To the question about prayer, he replied, "I pray for the good health of my family, for my grandchildren and for my fellowman. I have always tried to do my best for everybody, to be fair to everybody. But I have had problems with labor in my company. I worked hard for years to build up my business. Now with unionization, all they do is make demands. If you expect gratitude for all you do for people, you will be disappointed. I have done everything I can for people, but they lack appreciation." When asked how God was meaningful to his father and mother, he said, "My mother was born a Catholic. So was I. But after my father died, she drew away from the Catholic church. My mother had to scrub floors on her hands and knees, while the priest rode around in a big car. Later my mother joined the Eastern Star. My father was a 32nd degree Mason. Wherever there was a church near where we lived, my father joined it." To the question, "What religious idea is most important to you now?" he said, "To live up to the Golden Rule. That covers a multitude of sins. It's not hard to adhere to it if you are a Christian man." When asked to state three wishes, he said, "Good health, so that I can enjoy the fruits of my labor. To live long enough to see my grandchildren happily married. To have the undying respect of my fellow man, who I have been always trying to help and be good to."

The chaplain saw this man as having a psychophysiologic disorder, perhaps hypertension, and that his character structure was both paranoid and obsessive-compulsive. He was seen as rigid, inflexible and deprived, with latent hostility and constricted relations. He tries to hide his basic resentfulness and rationalizes his hostility. He demands gratitude, but probably gives little. His penurious, obstinate approach to people seems to be a defense against his insecurity, his fear of people and his emotional hunger. He seems to be afraid of closeness and emotions of tenderness and affection.

THE EDUCATIVE PROCESS

As the project developed over a three-year period, we have found ourselves moving more and more into a primary concern with education rather than research in any pure sense. It is well known that in studies such as this, it is impossible to control all of the variables. At Lutheran General Hospital, the psychiatric staff is comprised of men with quite different diagnostic styles. As a result, their reports must be seen from this perspective. The supervisors in the project also come from varying backgrounds and emphasize different things. Rather than fighting against the obvious, we have chosen to encourage these differences as an enriching aspect of training. The concern with instructors is excellence in teaching skills rather than some party line.

We have therefore, spent much time in evaluating the educational experience and have observed some frequent patterns in learning. Initially, the residents experience anxiety and resistance. This is due in part to the newness of the diagnostic categories and psychodynamic concepts.

Rather than proceeding at a slow pace, we chose to discuss each interview tape fully with the effect of "overloading" them with data. We believe that there is no way to avoid the awkward, stumbling experiences of initial learning. We have found that by repeated exposure to full diagnostic workups, students eventually begin to put things together and at a higher level than had we chosen to limit our early teaching to elementary distinctions. In the future a one-quarter course on psychodynamic concepts will be provided before the research project begins. This procedure has the disadvantage of introducing the more traditional two-level method of teaching, but since it will be immediately followed by the integrative approach, we are interested to see whether it will facilitate learning.

Another major source of anxiety for the resident is in rethinking his own religious views. To begin to see the way individuals reveal their own personalities through religious ideas and how emphasis on religious ideation is determined by forces of which the person is unaware opens up new avenues for self-reflection. This is an anxious time. Some of the residents at this point realize that the religious area of their lives has been a hiding place for unattended problems and so they seek therapeutic help. Allowing for individual variations, we have observed a general movement among the men to a more open, less critical and more perceptive religious experience with less need to impose their views on others.

We have also observed a process of acceleration in learning over the three-year period. Each class moves farther than the previous one. This we attribute to the increasing familiarity of the staff with teaching through this method and to the contagion of enthusiasm which the staff communicates.

One goal is to evaluate change in the residents as a result of the research project. We are not satisfied with religious questionnaires or the written and oral examinations. The variables of learning are great. It is difficult to determine how much of what a resident produces in an examination is integrated. The only real way to know for sure is to see the resident function in a clinical situation, but even here, the setting is not "natural" if an examiner is present. We are considering some long-range follow-up at a five-year interval as one other way to evaluate our work.

There are a number of other extensions of this project which we hope to explore. We want to do more to help the resident to learn how to adapt this method for parish work. We are interested in taking a fresh look at the question of denominational personality types, i.e. whether certain types of personalities will be drawn to a particular denomination and whether particular denominations contribute to the development of certain types of personalities. We also see some potential for training lay workers through some modification of this method to do a better job as pastoral assistants.

As evidenced by this study, we have found this method of teaching psychodynamics to have some distinct advantages over previously used methods. This is particularly true in two areas. It provides a greater opportunity for integration of psychological and theological training than two-level forms of teaching, and since it is done in a clinical setting, it combines both learning and service.

REFERENCES

Draper, Edgar: Psychiatry and Pastoral Care. Englewood Cliffs, N.J., Prentice-Hall, 1965.

Draper E., Meyer, G., Parsen, Z. and Samuelson, G.: The diagnostic value of religious ideation. Arch Gen Psychiatry, 13:202, 1965.

Eliade, Mircea: The Sacred and the Profane. New York, Harper and Row, 1957.

Freud, Sigmund: The future of an illusion. The Complete Psychological Works of Sigmund Freud. London, Hogarth Press, 1961.

Malinowski, Bronislaw: Anthropology. Encyclopaedia Britannica, 13th ed., Chicago, 1926.

Radcliffe-Brown, A. R.: Structure and Function in Primitive Society: Essays and Addresses. London, Cohen and West, 1952.

Ricoeur, Paul: Freud and Philosophy: An Essay on Interpretation. New Haven, Conn., Yale Univ. Press, 1970.

XIV

THE CHAPLAIN OF THE FUTURE:
Retrospect and Prospect

CARROLL A. WISE

THE institutional chaplain works in a context which is largely if not wholly dominated by professionals who have a scientific rather than religious orientation. Indeed, the institutional chaplain may suffer from severe isolation and may be subject to subtle pressures to move him gradually from his religious orientation. The fact is that the institutional chaplain, like the professional pastoral counselor, must have a dual orientation. He must be rooted and grounded in his religious faith, or else he has no ministry to offer. But he must also share in the scientific understanding of the kind of human problems represented by the patients in his institution. To be otherwise in a modern institution is to try to operate in a vacuum which soon sucks the chaplain into ineffective activity.

There are two aspects of the scientific atmosphere to consider. One is the tremendous contributions which have come from this field. These contributions have both aided the chaplain and have created problems for him.

The second aspect is the climate of protest against science today and what this may mean for the future and how it will continue to influence the relationship of pastors to scientific colleagues.

In the early days, as today, the doctor was and is the high priest of healing in institutions. Before an institutional ministry could be opened, physicians had to be sold on its desirability. This is still the case in many centers today. However, the protest movement against science, which began with Hiroshima, has now spread to the medical and behavioral sciences, and the high priests have been found by many to have feet of clay. (At the 1970 meeting of the American Association for the Advancement of Science, some of the sessions which had to do with psychiatry, medicine and the behavioral sciences could not be conducted because of the violent protests.)

As an illustration of the kind of protests which are being launched against the medical sciences, consider a recent book, *The American Health Empire: An Analysis of Power, Profits and Politics in American Medicine,* by Barbara and John Ehrenreich, published in 1971 by Random House. This book represents the thinking of a self-created think-tank called the Health Policy Advisory Center. It attacks large university-based medical centers, operated mostly by medical liberals. The authors say that these centers are not dedicated to medical care. Rather they are dedicated to ... three goals: increasing institutional profits and individual salaries; feeding medical research that often has only a tenuous relationship to any real medical needs; and insuring its own perpetuation by controlling medical education."*

The institutional minister must evaluate such criticisms in terms of the institution in which he works. He may have to minister to patients who share such views. He will have to deal with the influence such views have on the atmosphere of his institution, the effect they will have on medical scientists and his relationship to these men. He will have to decide whether he is to be a crusader, a supporter of the status quo or a creative, reconciling agent, bringing a ministry of reconciliation to each side of the conflict.

In short, the institutional ministry of the next few decades will be influenced greatly by the continued rise of scientific technocracy, by protests against this technocracy, and with this, close examination of the quality and costs of institutional care. The institutional chaplain cannot remain neutral and unconcerned with all of this. His task as a Christian pastor is that of being an agent of reconciliation, and he must learn how to do this.

BACKGROUND

Back in the early 1930's, some institutional chaplains became aware of (and were greatly influenced by) what came to be known as psychosomatic medicine. Dr. Flanders Dunbar, one of the

*From a review of the book in the Chicago *Tribune Book World,* January 24, 1971, p. 1.

leaders of this approach, was also the medical director of the Council for Clinical Training, having come into the movement in the middle 1920's when she came to Worcester as one of Anton Boisen's students. She had a tremendous positive influence on the thinking of many in those days. But the term "psychosomatic medicine" was really poor nomenclature for the underlying philosophy of this approach. Essentially it is grounded on an organismic view of life, a view which takes partial views, such as the biological, the chemical, the social and others, up into a view of the organism as a whole in relationship to its total environment.

This philosophy was not new. It had some roots in Greek medicine, and has some demonstration in the Bible. Today another word has come into popular use, for it has been discovered what man does to his environment and what in turn the environment does to man. The word today is *ecology,* and we have been forced into an awareness of this through the many ways in which man is polluting and otherwise destroying his environment, and how this in turn is destroying man. Some hospitals have developed on the basis of the principle of *human ecology,* an attempt to look at the whole man in relation to his total environment.

Such an approach is native to the pastor, for the goal of religious faith has long been stated as wholeness. Religious faith has been concerned with the relation of man's spirit to both his internal and external environments, including in both dimensions the manifestation of the living God. The institutional chaplain has a responsibility to place himself in the center of any movement within the health sciences or professions which is seeking to deal with man in his wholeness. This is one of the waves of the future in chaplaincy work.

GENERAL SYSTEM THEORY*

Related to this is a theoretical approach within sciences which

*Two good general introductions to General System Theory will be found in Ludwig Von Bertalanffy: *General System Theory.* New York, George Braziller, 1968, and in Ludwig Von Bertalanffy: *Robots, Men and Minds.* New York, George Braziller, 1967. Applications of this approach to marriage and family therapy will be found in Greene, Bernard L.: *A Clinical Approach to Marital Problems.* Springfield, Thomas, 1970, and in Olson, David H.: Marital and family therapy: Integrative review and critique. *Journal of Marriage and the Family,* November, 1970, p. 501.

has come to be known as general system theory. General system theory is a movement within the natural, biological and behavioral sciences which seeks to relate the facts and theories of the various sciences into a unified system of thought. The organismic view points to the need to understand man as a whole. General system seeks to relate knowledge presented by the discrete sciences into a unified theory. It has philosophical roots and mathematical methodology. It is rapidly becoming the means of interdisciplinary communication among the sciences. Theology in the past has tried to come to terms with discrete sciences or scientific theories. Theology of the future will have to come to terms with this new way of thinking in science.

The institutional chaplain of the future will have to know something about general system theory for two purposes:

1. He will need it as a basis of communication with other disciplines.

2. He has a creative opportunity in the task of relating general system theory to theology. Theology cannot ignore general systems any more than it could ignore Darwin or Freud. In order to avoid playing word games, clinical experiences will have to be at the core of any creative integrating process, and the institutional chaplain, along with the professional pastoral therapist, are the two persons in the theological field who have this clinical data. A big task is being thrust upon chaplains by the intellectual developments of the immediate past and the immediate future.

Another aspect of ministry related to the scientific atmosphere is the clarification of the identity as institutional chaplaincy in relation to the growing practice of psychotherapy. In the 1930's psychotherapy was largely in the hands of the psychiatrists, but other professions were moving in. Freud published his famous book on lay analysis in 1926. One of the early issues in clinical pastoral education was whether ministers were being trained as psychiatrists or clergymen. Often it was not heard when it was said that training was being given in the understanding of the human condition so that the clergy could function better as clergy. This was not heard because of the assumption that if the pastor had his theology he did not need anything else to do this job. This attitude is still found in some quarters today.

In the intervening years there has been tremendous development both within the concept of the ministry and the field of psychotherapy, so that today the medical profession no longer has the exclusive rights. Some physicians have aided and abetted this development, feeling with Freud that medical training is not essential for the psychotherapist, providing he uses medical consultation in his work. Pastoral psychotherapy is emerging into a profession that will have to be taken into account.

The situation today has many ambiguities and opportunities. In it there are a number of challenges for the pastor, and particularly the institutional chaplain and the professional pastoral therapist. One should become honest, discard the term "pastoral counseling," and recognize that what chaplains are carrying on is pastoral psychotherapy. If psychotherapy is conceived as the healing of a person, or as changing motivation or behavior, then preaching is a form of psychotherapy. The visit of the pastor at a bedside is a form of psychotherapy. Or to reverse matters, the work of the secular therapist is a form of religious ministry, and is so accepted by some. Some secular psychotherapists are moving in on areas which have been traditionally those of the pastor, for example, the ministry to dying patients.

In addition to first becoming honest, chaplains secondly need to face the question as to whether what is being done is good or bad psychotherapy, and to use some criteria other than "getting at feelings." Damage can be done to persons in some situations by getting at feelings. In the third place, some radical thinking must be done about which of the numerous so-called new forms of psychotherapy are appropriate for the Christian pastor. Some of these are grounded on a concept of man which is totally incongruous with the Christian concept of man. It is the style today to grab at a sense of professional security by adopting old errors under the guise of a new approach. Fourth, chaplains must work harder at relating (not integrating) psychological theory with theological theory and practice, as one means of solidifying our pastoral identity. Fifth, chaplains need to accept and develop the principle of consultation with specialists from other fields and to learn what such consultation means in terms of developing our own identities.

There is another aspect of the contribution of science which is having its impact on the chaplaincy and will have more impact in the future. This is the body of tremendous medical advances which have been made and others which are just over the horizon and the serious ethical issues which these raise. In being called upon to speak to these ethical issues, the pastor or institutional chaplain is being called back to the ethical roots of the Judeo-Christian faith. He is being called upon to become an expert in ethical understanding and practice, in the communication of this to all sorts and conditions of men, and in doing the pastoral job of helping persons relate this to crucial experiences in a healing manner. This may mean adding some significant dimensions to his training.*

THE THERAPEUTIC COMMUNITY†

There is another aspect of the identity of the pastor, inside of an institution or outside. In recent decades there has been more awareness, and the significance of this community reaching back into the roots of faith in the Old Testament, continuing in the New Testament and down through the tradition of the church. This community had a saving, healing or therapeutic function. In recent years a somewhat similar consciousness has been forming within the secular community around the concept of "the therapeutic community." Again the dual orientation of the pastor becomes both an opportunity and a challenge, for he must learn how to relate the healing work of the community of faith to healing processes within the secular community.

From either point of view, healing may be said to be the result of forces and potentials which arise from within the person, but this can happen only in a community which facilitates their

*See Lyons, Catherine: *Organ Transplants, The Moral Issues.* Philadelphia Westminister Press, 1970, and Mann, Kenneth: *Deadline for Survival: A Survey of Moral Issues in Science and Medicine.* New York, Seabury Press, 1970.

†Two works dealing with the problems of the therapeutic community are the following: Leighton, Alexander; Clausen, John A., and Wilson, Robert n.: *Explorations in Social Psychiatry.* New York, Basic Books, 1957, and Jones, Maxwell: *Beyond the Therapeutic Community.* New Haven, Yale Univ. Press, 1968. See also Duff, Raymond S. and Hollingshead, August B.: *Sickness and Society.* New York, Harper and Row, 1968.

emergence. The institutional chaplain cannot be content to confine himself to one-to-one patient care. He must also be concerned, along with other professionals, with the impact of the entire community on the healing process.

Looking now at the larger community as part of the context in which chaplains work, all are fully aware of the revolutionary forces at work today throughout the world and the need for social and political change. The place of the institutional chaplain in the process of social change is a complex problem, not to be answered by any easy formula and not answered in the same manner by all pastors. Certainly one contribution which the institutional chaplain can make is the clarification, for the church and for the community, of conditions which contribute to the problems which he faces within the institution. This is in line with previous comments on human ecology. Chaplains should be viewed as agents of prevention as well as agents of cure.

Another contribution is to emphasize the crucial significance of persons in the process of social change. Under some conditions the change of structures can bring harm to persons. Change in itself, either in the individual or society, may be either regressive or redemptive, and the institutional minister is in a position to speak to the human values in this process.

What should be said about the institutional chaplain and his relationship to the church at large? In the early days of this movement the lines of the church were clear and distinct. Today they are blurred and confused. Tomorrow what?

This provides an opportunity. The institutional chaplain knows that the renewal of the church will not come by change of structure or form, though such changes may be needed. The renewal of the church, or healing of the church, will be the result of the emergence of a revitalized religious faith. It is a matter of spirit, not form. The chaplain's daily work ought to be contributing greatly to this end.

Pastors in the community have needs, too. They indeed have their problems today. For them, chaplains can become part of the answer to the question as to who is to be the pastor to pastors. They need fellowship, and consultation on pastoral care. The practice of conducting educational programs for local pastors began long ago and needs to continue and be developed. It would seem that there is no better place to establish a pastoral counseling service where clergy can make referrals and seek consultation, than in the institutions in which chaplains serve, especially if these are church-related institutions.

CONTRIBUTIONS OF CPE TO THE CHURCH

One of the contributions of the chaplain to the church is through clinical pastoral education (CPE). Great strides have been made in clinical pastoral education since its beginning. It has made and is making unique contributions to theological education, to interprofessional relationships of the clergy and to the ministry of those who have participated in it. Indeed it is doubtful if the institutional chaplaincy would have developed to the place that it is today without the contribution of clinical pastoral education.

Today a major need is an examination of what clinical pastoral education is and how it should be done. For example, here is a sentence out of a report from an accredited center and supervisor on one student: "He was exposed to the kind of therapy which uses desensitization, reality therapy, transactional analysis and perhaps combinations of these and others including behavioral modification."

All this in one quarter! As a seminary professor who has a long history in clinical pastoral education, the author wants to say that this kind of statement represents a serious perversion of the basic aims and purposes of CPE.

Another influence which is forcing some reevaluation of CPE is the rise of the pastoral counseling movement and the growth of American Association of Pastoral Counselors. The two national organizations representing these movements each have their distinctive functions and should not be identified nor merged. But there is a need to meet for fellowship and the discussion of issues. One of these issues is the relationship between CPE and training in pastoral counseling on the professional level. Some people are identifying these. They are not to be identified in basic philosophy, method or goal. Each has its distinctive aspects. One task in the immediate future is to work at clarifying these issues.

In the process, there may be some improvements in both areas of training.

Much more could be said about these issues. They are subordinate, however, to the central reason for the existence of the institutional chaplain, that is, the pastoral care of patients or inmates of his institution. In the early days of this movement the emphasis was on trying to formulate the general outlines and procedures of pastoral care.

Today it is somewhat different, though the early problems have not been entirely resolved. Anyone looking at the program of a conference of hospital chaplains, particularly the titles of the papers and workshops, cannot but be impressed with the many and diverse aspects of pastoral care. This adds up to the one line of development which the future will take. In addition to the generalized problems of pastoral care, many institutional chaplains have already become and will further become specialists in the ministry to persons suffering from specific forms of human infirmities. This is already happening in some institutions which have a sufficiently large staff of men in the pastoral care field.

DEALING WITH DEATH

But there are deeper dimensions of pastoral care which cut across either generalized or specialized work and are essential to each. One illustration is the concern which has emerged in recent years around the experiences of bereavement and dying.*

The first of these dimensions is that the pastor, regardless of the type of person to whom he is ministering, must be inwardly and deeply comfortable with that person and the problems he represents. When it comes to experiences of suffering and his possible death, he will be somewhat of a phony in ministering to persons facing these problems unless he has come to terms with his

---

*Freud, Sigmund: Mourning and Melancholia. *Collected Papers,* vol. IV, London, Hogarth, 1924. Lindemann, Erich: Symptomatology and management of acute grief. *American Journal of Psychiatry, 101:*141, 1944. Ross, Elisabeth Kubler: *On Death and Dying.* New York, Macmillan, 1969. Schoenberg, Bernard, Carr, Arthur C., Peretz, David, and Jutscher, Austin H. (Eds.): *Loss and Grief.* New York, Columbia University Press, 1970.

Toward a Creative Chaplaincy

own suffering and death. And coming to terms with his own actual suffering and potential death is not a matter of theologizing about them intellectually. It is a matter of penetrating beneath the tremendous superstructure of personality into the deep substructure where there is a tremendously potent force which brings the profound assurance, not that some day we shall overcome suffering and find immortality, but that today we are participating in a dimension of life which is eternal.

This is the New Testament answer, this is the answer of the Christian mystics, and of others who have arrived at the same experience by a diverse route. It is the answer which many young people are seeking today in the psychedelic experience. Without a profound sense of inner certainty and personal assurance, perhaps the best one can do is to help a patient die somewhat peacefully.

Consider too the works of Dr. Robert Jay Lifton,* a research psychiatrist at Yale University. Lifton has studied the survivors of Hiroshima, the Chinese Revolution, the military establishment, the youth culture and other such phenomena. He seems to have gotten beneath the superstructure of personality to the deep substructure. He sees in man, universally, a driving urge toward a sense of immortality in the face of biological death. He understands the great social and political movements of our day in the light of this urgent drive toward a sense of immortality.

The implications of Lifton's thought are many. But one important message is simply the importance of meeting the threat of suffering and death personally so that chaplains have a firm assurance within to offer patients. The other alternative is that chaplains pursue the institutional ministry as a way of compensating for their own profound inner lacks and fears and so will not be able to deal with the profound issues facing the sufferer. Chaplains will be unintentionally aided and abetted in this by the physician who over tranquilizes his patients, and thereby robs them of the power of autonomy and strength to face their suffering, and hence

---

*The major works of Robert Jay Lifton are the following: *Death in Life: Survivors of Hiroshima.* New York, Random House, 1968; *Revolutionary Immortality: The Chinese Cultural Revolution.* New York, Random House, 1968; *Boundaries: Psychological Man in Revolution.* New York, Random House, 1969; *The Broken Connection.* To be Published. See also, Harris, George T.: The politics of immortality: A conversation with Robert Jay Lifton, In *Psychology Today,* 4:6; 70, 1970.

tends to reduce them from human beings to something less than that.

In the next breath it should be pointed out that the church has had its own form of tranquilizers also. Perhaps all those working with any form of human suffering should come to terms with their own anxieties about suffering and death, and their own desires to make things as easy as possible without sufficient concern for those profound possessions of the human spirit which come only through difficult discipline.

Another dimension of the pastoral ministry which deserves much development in the future is the meaning of nonverbal communication. Or to put it differently, the Christian faith is a religion of the Incarnation, the Word becoming flesh. The principle of the Incarnation is the deepest form of communication of faith. There are times in the ministry when words are so ineffective and useless. At all times the chaplain's words have to be undergirded by the reality of his faith. Often chaplains make but little distinction between what they do and what other helpers do for human beings. Chaplains become genuine pastors only when in their relationship they communicate something of the redemptive love of God. Speech may aid in this, but speech without the inner reality is useless and may be harmful.

There is a tendency on the part of many who stress relationship to denigrate knowledge. There is also a tendency on the part of those who stress knowledge to ignore relationships. Within the entire ministry, chaplains need to develop the ways in which both the capacity for knowledge and the capacity for empathy are enhanced. In the light of the tremendous potential for development of the institutional chaplaincy, some of which has been touched on here and some not, and in the light of increased need for knowledge on the part of anyone dealing with persons, the day is coming when many institutional chaplains will have to have training on the doctoral level. This has many implications which need discussion. In no way should it exclude an emphasis on empathy, nor does it need to do so. In this work there is no substitute for either knowledge or empathy. In the next decades there will be some discovery or rediscovery of aspects of persons that will make what is called depth psychology today look a bit superficial. Institutional chaplains will have to keep abreast of the developments.

In many ways, the course of future developments in society and in this profession lie hidden from view. This should be seen as a challenge. Chaplains have a tremendous opportunity to contribute to the renewal of religious faith as they fulfill their ministry to those patients under their care, to their families and to the larger community. For this ministry, chaplains will need to be rooted deeply in the Biblical faith, to be thoroughly grounded in essential modern knowledge of persons and to have come into the possession of their own being which gives meaning and assurance in the face of human suffering and death.

Appendix

THE DEPARTMENT OF PASTORAL CARE
LUTHERAN GENERAL HOSPITAL

THE Pastoral Care Department has been developed as an integral part of the hospital to assure recognition and treatment of the spiritual as well as physical needs. This department cooperates closely with all religious groups to assure that the patient has the kind of ministry he prefers or which is best suited to his personal background.

The department is administered by a director, who is assisted by associate directors in the areas of in-patient ministry, out-patient counseling and education.

The following is a brief description of the activities and programs of the Department of Pastoral Care.

I. In-Patient Ministry

A. A chaplain is in the hospital 24 hours a day, seven days a week and can be reached by having the operator page him.

B. A chaplain is assigned to each clinical area of the hospital and is available for referrals or requests for visitation by any hospital staff member.

C. The chaplain will attempt to make initial visits on all patients in the hospital to offer a ministry. The Pastoral Care Office telephones notification of admission to the appropriate parish clergyman when a patient professes membership in a specific parish or congregation.

D. The chaplain visits critical patients daily, makes preoperation visits on all surgical patients the evening prior to surgery and is notified at the time of any expirations in the hospital. While he attempts to visit as many patients as possible during a day, he does appreciate any staff person calling his attention to any patients in particular need of pastoral care.

E. Common pastoral functions are carried out by the chaplain in the following cases:

    1. He is called for all expirations. He will notify the appropriate clergymen for the last rites, if these are indicated. He will meet

with the family and minister to them in their grief. He will coordinate some of the necessary details, i.e. signing of release of remains and autopsy permit (where indicated) and giving personal effects to the family.

2. He is called for emergency baptisms. If time permits, he will notify the appropriate clergymen. If not, he will perform the Sacrament of Baptism.
3. He is called where a patient and/or family seems to be particularly distressed.
4. He is available to the Emergency Department for any emergencies that require or could use pastoral care.
5. He administers Holy Communion upon request, and when patient's parish pastor is unable to fulfill such request.
6. In his rounds he demonstrates the love of Christ through personal integrity, warm, nonpossessive care and interest in staff and patients.

F. Chaplains are involved in several special areas of the hospital where structured programs or specific needs are present. In addition to more common functions of pastoral ministry, the chaplain has other responsibilities in these areas. Some of these are as follows:

1. Rehabilitation unit. The chaplain assists in the leadership of group meetings for families of stroke patients, the leadership of group meetings of patients, in the assessment of patient needs and in appropriate contributions to the care and treatment of patients.
2. Ecology unit. The chaplain participates in the diagnosis and treatment of patients, on both group and individual basis, who are experiencing excessive somatization of emotional stress.
3. Coronary unit. The chaplain is responsible, with a social worker, for the leadership of daily group meetings with heart attack patients.
4. Adolescent unit. The chaplain participates in "talk-out" group meetings with teenagers.
5. Relative surgical waiting area. One chaplain's prime responsibility is to be available to the families of surgical patients each day and to consult with the recovery room upon request or need of the family.
6. Psychiatric units. Chaplains participate in the leadership of various therapeutic groups, including weekly religious discussion group meetings.

G. The chaplain will often use the Ecology Memo on the patient's chart to share his evaluations and make recommendations for the care of that patient. He will share these verbally, also, as he works with the medical staff.

H. Formal worship. Worship services are held in the chapel for patients and personnel. Patients need permission from their physician to attend. These services are conducted by hospital chaplains but are open to persons of all faiths. These services are about 15 minutes long. Patients are welcome in hospital garb.

I. Visiting clergymen from the community may report to the pastoral care office before making visits on patients. They are given an identification name tag and have access to a file of all patients in the hospital. We suggest that they check with the nursing station before making a visit. It is a policy of the department to assist and encourage in every possible way, the ongoing pastoral relationship of the parish minister, priest or rabbi.

II. Out-Patient Ministry

A new division within the Department is called the Community Pastoral Counseling and Consultation Center. It has two functions. One is to see out-patients for pastoral counseling. These may be referred from the hospital staff or from pastors or others in the community. Individuals may come without referral. The second function is consultation with pastors in regard to pastoral problems in the community. Appointments may be made through the Pastoral Care Office. There are fees for counseling services. These are discussed in the initial interview.

III. Education

There are various types of educational programs and seminars which are conducted by the department.

A. Clinical pastoral education is a learning process for clergymen set in an institutional framework whereby the student is helped, via the pastoral office, to minister with better understanding to persons. The program provides a setting in which the pastor may develop deeper awareness of the theological concerns of persons in crisis, and where he might integrate his theology more meaningfully with life. Students receive individual and group supervision by certified chaplain-supervisors in the department. The department has three programs which are accredited by the Association for Clinical Pastoral Education.

1. One-year residency. Six pastors spend a year in an accredited, supervised program of clinical pastoral education. The program

runs from July 1 to June 30. There is a yearly stipend given by the hospital. During their year these men function as hospital chaplains, attend daily seminars and receive supervision. Many of these men return to the parish ministry following their year and some accept positions as institutional chaplains.

2. Three-month program. An 11-week program is conducted in spring, summer, and fall. There is a tuition fee. Mean and bachelor housing are furnished by the hospital. Each program accepts six pastors and/or seminarians. They function as hospital chaplains, attend daily seminars, and receive supervision.

3. Part-time program is designed for area parish ministry. Six pastors spend 16 hours per week for 30 weeks. There is a tuition fee. Their clinical experience occurs in their parish setting. They receive supervision.

B. Part-time internship. Each year the hospital has four interns from a seminary who split their time between a parish and the hospital. The intern spends three days ministering in the assigned parish. The hospital and parishes share the cost of the program. The students receive individual and group supervision.

C. Divine Word Seminary. Each year the senior class at Divine Word Roman Catholic Seminary, Techny, Illinois, spend 11 weeks at the hospital in a supervised C.P.E. (nonaccredited) program. While at the hospital, the student priests function as hospital chaplains, attend daily seminars, receive supervision and conduct Mass on Sundays.

D. Intern-vicar program. The hospital participates with the Lutheran School of Theology and St. Mary of the Lake Seminary in a program for Chicago area seminary interns and vicars. The department provides a staff person to meet monthly with a group of interns and their pastors.

E. Various seminars/courses. Through the year the department conducts groups, institutes, seminars and classes. These seminars are open to clergymen of all faiths.

F. Pre-Marital Institute is an institute for young couples about to be married and is conducted six times a year (January, March, May, July, September, and November). Each institute consists of four Monday-evening sessions. A physician, a social worker, a psychiatrist, a financier and a pastor lead discussions in the various aspects of marriage. A fee is charged to cover the costs of books and inventories used.

IV. Research

The department is committed to research in areas of pastoral care. The department has a full-time and two part-time research consultants. The results of much of their research is published.

INDEX

A

Adaptation to fear of death, 52-54
Al-anon, 94, 95
Alcoholic patient, 87-95
  dealing with, 87
  definition of, 89, 90
  progressive symptom chart, 88
  symptoms, 88 (fig.)
  talking to the, 92-94
Alcoholics Anonymous, 94, 95
The American Health Empire: An Analysis of Power, Profits and Politics in American Medicine, 140
The Art of Ministering to the Ill, ix
Association for Clinical Pastoral Education, 89

B

Background of the chaplain, 140-141
Bickel, A. O., v
Board of Governors of the Lutheran Institute of Human Ecology, xiv
Boisen, A., 86, ix, 130, 141
Bruder, E., 78, 86
Bruehl, R. G., 15, 21

C

Cabot, R., ix
Carr, A. C., 147
Chaplain
  enabler, 3
  mediator, 3
  mobilizer, 3
  role of (*see* specific tasks)
  what he is, 5, 6
  what he is not, 3, 4
The Christian Pastor, x, 75
Clausen, J. A., 144

Clinical pastoral education, 146
  contribution to the church, 146, 147
Communication, importance of in rehabilitation unit, 57, 58
Community pastoral counseling center, 118-127
  background of the center, 120-122
  referral reasons, 124-127
  who uses the center, 122-124
Coronary patients
  group meetings of, 42-49
    didactic-therapeutic sessions, 43
    experience of patients, 45-47
    goals and format, 44, 45
    medical consultation, 45
    response of patients, 47-49
Crisis
  surgery, 35-37
  types of, 25, 26
Crisis visit, 22
  definition of, 22
  issues to consider, 30-32
    group ministry, 31
    perception of need, 31
    results, 32
    unknowns, 30
    skill involved, 30
Curran, C. A., 15, 21

D

Death
  dealing with, 147-150
  fear of, 49
    adaption to, 52-54
    denial of, 49
    dependence on others, 51, 52
    depression created, 52
Denial of fear of death, 49-51
Department of Pastoral Care at Lutheran

General Hospital, xiii, xiv, 151-155
Dependence on others through fear of death, 51, 52
Depression created by fear of death, 52
The Diagnostic Value of Religious Ideation, 130, 131
Dicks, R., ix
Draper, E., 130, 138
Duff, R. S., 144
Dunbar, F., 140

E

Education program, 153-155
Ehrenreich, B., 140
Ehrenreich, J., 140
Eliade, M., 138
Emotion and Illness, 63-77
    chaplain's role in treatment, 70-73
    resolution of, 68, 69
Enabler, chaplain as, 3
The Exploration of the Inner World, ix

F

Fichter, J. H., 21
Fletcher, P., 65
Freud, S., 138, 142, 147
Future, chaplain of the, 139-150

G

General system theory, 141-144
    purpose of chaplain knowing, 142
Glock, C. Y., 21
God, psychiatric patient's relationship to, 80-85
Greene, B. L., 141

H

"Hallway ministry," 28, 29
Harris, G. T., 148
Hartung, B. M., 21, v
Health producing forces, 105, 106
A History of the Cure of Souls, ix
Hollingshead, A. B., 144
Holst, L. E., v
Hospital

crisis visit, 22-32
visit
    function of, 16
    initial call (*see* Initial call)
    study conducted on, 17
    work with patients, 6-10
Hospital chaplain versus parish pastor, 106-109
Hospital staff, chaplain's relationship with, 11
Howe, R., 82

I

Illness
    changing concepts of, 63-65
    emotional related to physical, 65-67
    factors contributing to, 65-68
    how to deal with, 6-10
In-patient ministry, 151-153
Initial call, 15-21
    "pre-op" call, 19
    suggestions for improvement, 20
    tension of, 18-20
Interview, religious as a method of teaching
    psychodynamics, 128-138
Ivery, A. E., 21

J

Jesus and Logotherapy, 85
Jones, M., 144
Jutscher, A. H., 147

K

Keller, J. E., v
Kurtz, H. P., v

L

Leighton, A., 144
Leslie, R. L., v
Leslie, R. R., 85
Lifton, R. J., 148
Lindemann, E., 144
Lyons, C., 144

M

Malinowski, B., 129, 138
Mann, K., 144

McHolland, J. D., 15, 16, 21
McNeil, J. T., ix
Mediator
  chaplain as, 3
  patient to patient, 10, 11
Meilburg, A. L., x
Meyer, G., 138
The Minister and Doctor Meet, x
Ministering to the Physically Sick, x
Miracle of Dialogue, The, 82
Mobilizer, chaplain as, 3

N

Nasheim, H. S., v
Nordgren, A., v
North American Association of Alcohol-
  ism Programs, 89

O

Oates, W., x, 75
Olson, D., 141
Out-patient ministry, 153

P

Parsen, Z., 138
Parish pastor
  collaboration with chaplain, 116, 117
  education, orientation to hospital,
    113-116
  hospital calls by, 109-111
  hospital chaplain and, 105-117
  hospital chaplain as a unit with,
    112-117
  information gathered on patient,
    112, 113
Part of the healing team, 15
Pastoral Care in a Historial Perspective,
  ix
Patient
  alcoholic (*see* alcoholic patient)
  chaplain as mediator with other
    patients, 10
  communication with the outside world
    through the chaplain, 12
  coronary (*see* Coronary patient)
  creating relationship with 15, 16
  not needing chaplain, 37, 38, 39

rehabilitation unit, 55-62 (*see also*
  Rehabilitation unit)
Psychiatric (*see* Psychiatric patient)
study of those requesting chaplain, 17
surgical (*see* Surgical patient)
work with, 6-10
Peretz, D., 147
"Pre-op" visit, 27, 28
Program
  Department of Pastoral Care Lutheran
    General Hospital, 151-155
  education, 153-155
  in-patient, 151-155
  out-patient, 158
Psychodynamics
  research project in pastoral counseling,
    128-130
    assumptions, 130, 131
    case summaries, 133-136
    educative process, 136-138
    questionnaire, 131-133
    taught by religious interview, 128-138
Psychiatry and Pastoral Care, 130
Psychiatric patient
  case study, 79, 80
  pastoral care of, 78-86
  relationship to God, 80-85
  staff involvement, 85, 86

R

Radcliffe-Brown, A. R., 138
Ree, A. J., v
Rehabilitation unit, 55-62
  adjustment to disability, 55
  concept explained, 56, 57
  dealing with patient depression and
    fear, 58-62
  staff communication, 57, 58
Religion In Illness and Health, x
Richardson, E. A., v
Ricoeur, P., 130, 138
Robin, S., 21
Role of chaplain, 18
Roos, P., 21
Ross, E. K., 147

S

Samuelson, G., 138

Schoenberg, B., 147
Sherzer, C. J., x
Spiritual Therapy
Surgery, work in, 26, 27
Surgical crisis
 feeling of patient undergoing surgery,
  39
 response of chaplain
Surgical patient
 financial fears of, 39-41
 need for chaplain, 33-35
Staff
 common concern to, 96, 97, 98
 hospital
  chaplain's relationship with, 11
 ministry to, 96-104
 opportunities for ministry, 98-101
 psychiatric, 85, 86
Staff ministry
 underlying assumptions, 101-104

T

Team
 chaplain as member of therapeutic,
  73-76
 part of the healing, 15
Therapeutic community, 144-146

Therapeutic team, chaplain as member,
 73-76
Thurneysen, E., 15, 21
Travis, A. E., 15, 16, 21
Treatment, chaplain's role in, 70

U

Understanding Your Emotional Problems, 65

V

Von Bertalanffy, L., 141

W

Wagner, W., v
Weatherhead, L., 54
Westberg, G., x, 15, 21, 75
Williams, B., 54
Wilson, R. N., 144
Wise, C. A., v, x, xi, 15, 21, 139
Whitley, O. R., 18, 21
Work with patients, 6-10

Y

Young, R. K., x